CRITICAL READING SERIES

DAREDEVILS

21 Stories of Extraordinary Daring—with Exercises for Developing Reading Comprehension and Critical Thinking Skills

Henry Billings
Melissa Billings

JAMESTOWN PUBLISHERS
a division of NTC/Contemporary Publishing Group
Lincolnwood, Illinois USA

ISBN 0-89061-114-9

Published by Jamestown Publishers,
a division of NTC/Contemporary Publishing Group, Inc.
4255 West Touhy Avenue,
Lincolnwood (Chicago), Illinois 60712-1975, U.S.A.

01 02 03 04 05 06 VL12 11 10 9 8 7 6 5 4

DAREDEVILS

CONTENTS

UNIT THREE

To the Student

At one time or another, most of us are daredevils. We know that we really don't need to take this foolish chance or try that dangerous stunt. Despite that knowledge, we choose to risk our safety just for the thrill of trying something that others would be afraid to attempt. Most of us outgrow our desire to prove ourselves in these dangerous ways. However, the people you will read about in this book never outgrew their need for—and enjoyment of—adventure and risk-taking

Each lesson will introduce you to a different person or group of people who routinely risk their safety and sometimes even their lives. Some of these daredevils will seem courageous and worthy of imitation. You will decide that others are simply reckless and foolhardy. But no matter what you think of them, you can be sure of one thing. They don't care about your opinion. They do what they want to do in spite of criticism, discouragement, pain, and danger. In fact, the more difficult the task is, the more likely it is that they will accomplish it or die trying.

All the articles tell about actual events recorded in books and newspapers. As you read and enjoy them, you will also be developing your reading skills. *Daredevils* is for students who already read fairly well but who want to read faster and to increase their understanding of what they read. If you complete the 21 lessons—reading the articles and completing the exercises—you will surely increase your reading speed and improve your reading comprehension and critical thinking skills. Also, because these exercises include items of the types often found on state and national tests, learning how to complete them will prepare you for tests you may have to take in the future.

How to Use This Book

About the Book. *Daredevils* contains three units, each of which includes seven lessons. Each lesson begins with an article about an unusual event, person, or group. The article is followed by a group of four reading comprehension exercises and a set of three critical thinking exercises. The reading comprehension exercises will help you understand the article. The critical thinking exercises will help you think about what you have read and how it relates to your own experience.

At the end of each lesson, you will also have the opportunity to give your personal response to some aspect of the article and then to assess how well you understood what you read.

The Sample Lesson. Working through the sample lesson, the first lesson in the book, with your class or group will demonstrate how a lesson is organized. The sample lesson explains how to complete the exercises and score your answers. The correct answers for the sample exercises and sample scores are printed in lighter type. In some cases, explanations of the correct answers are given. The explanations will help you understand how to think through these question types.

If you have any questions about how to complete the exercises or score them, this is the time to get the answers.

Working Through Each Lesson. Begin each lesson by looking at the photographs and reading the captions. Before you read, predict what you think the article will be about. Then read the article.

Sometimes your teacher may decide to time your reading. Timing helps you keep track of and increase your reading speed. If you have been timed, enter your reading time in the box at the end of the lesson. Then use the Words-per-Minute Table to find your reading speed, and record your speed on the Reading Speed graph at the end of the unit.

Next complete the Reading Comprehension and Critical Thinking exercises. The directions for each exercise will tell you how to mark your answers. When you have finished all four Reading Comprehension exercises, use the answer key provided by your teacher to check your work. Follow the directions after each exercise to find your score. Record your Reading Comprehension scores on the graph at the end of each unit. Then check your answers to the Author's Approach, Summarizing and Paraphrasing, and Critical Thinking exercises. Fill in the Critical Thinking chart at the end of each unit with your evaluation of your work and comments about your progress.

At the end of each unit you will also complete a Compare/Contrast chart. The completed chart will help you see what the articles have in common, and it will give you an opportunity to explore your own attitudes about risk-taking and daredevils.

SAMPLE LESSON

VOLCANO WATCHERS

It was early afternoon on January 14, 1993. A United Nations team of scientists carefully made its way down into the crater of the Galeras volcano in Colombia. Galeras seemed to be a safe volcano. It issued few rumblings. Little gas was venting from the crater. And there had been almost no swelling of the mountain. None of the volcano watchers suspected that molten rock had pushed its way up into the volcano and was ready to erupt.

2 The eruption came at 1:40 P.M. It was not a large blast. It did not threaten the nearby town of Pasto. But for the team inspecting the volcano, it meant big trouble. Andrew McFarlane was one of the scientists on the scene. First, he heard a loud boom. Then he looked up to see what was going on. "I could see a dark cloud rising over the top of the crater," he said. "It was hard to tell how serious it was, but we knew it wasn't good, and we started running."

3 Within seconds, blocks of hot rocks began to fall all around the scientists. One block nicked McFarlane. He stumbled and fell several times in an effort to reach safe

Scientists work near the lava tube on the Kilauea Volcano in Hawaii.

ground. Others did the same. "I saw one of the Colombians get basically crushed by [a block of hot rock]," said McFarlane. "It seemed very unlikely that any of us were going to get out alive."

4 Luckily, local Red Cross rescue workers rushed to the scene. They saved the life of McFarlane, who by then could no longer move. He was suffering from burns, bruises, a gashed forehead, and a small skull fracture. Six other members of the UN team, however, could not be saved. The Galeras eruption caused the most deaths for volcano watchers since 1952, when nine watchers died in Japan.

5 Andrew McFarlane was later asked what his thoughts were while he was scrambling for his life. Had he regretted his decision to become a volcano watcher? Hadn't he "sort of asked for it" by choosing such a dangerous job? "Yeah," McFarlane answered. "A lot of thoughts like that were going through my mind.... I was thinking things like, boy, my dad's really going to be upset if I get killed up here."

6 Less than two months later, disaster struck again. In Ecuador, a volcano erupted on March 9. Two young men from a research center in Quito decided—on their own—to film the debris. It was a foolish idea. The director of the Institute knew the volcano was still active and could turn deadly. The film simply wasn't worth the risk. So he radioed the pair to "get out as soon as possible." The message either did not get through or the men ignored it. On March 12, the volcano erupted again. It was just a small eruption. But it was enough to kill both young men.

7 The two men killed in Ecuador had little experience. They made a rash choice that cost them their lives. Some of the people killed in Colombia, on the other hand, were old pros. They knew the risks involved, yet they ventured into the crater anyway. They hoped to find out if Galeras was just blowing off a little steam or really getting ready to go. After all, a major eruption would have endangered the lives of the 300,000 residents in Pasto. Like all

Volcanologists Jack Lockwood and Tara Moulds monitor the activity of a volcano at the Hawaiian Volcano National Park.

good volcano watchers, the Galeras team tried to balance the risks against the knowledge to be gained. Sadly, in this case, the balance was tipped against them.

8 Most of the time the risks are not that great. Scott Rowland said, "Honestly, I think that my daily commute to the office on my bicycle is more dangerous than working out in the field on a volcano." And in a way he is right. Only a handful of volcanologists have died in the line of duty. Over the past 50 years, the number has totaled 27.

9 Volcanoes, meanwhile, kill lots of other folks. In the 1980s, 28,500 people died from volcanic blasts. Volcano watchers try to cut down the number of such deaths. They check each gurgle or burp a volcano makes. Much of their work is done with instruments placed on the volcano. But some of it must be done in person on the rim of a crater.

10 Predicting when a volcanc is going to blow is not a precise science. Our knowledge in this field is not complete. The inner workings of a volcano remain a mystery. Maurice Kraft put it this way. "We still have no general theory of volcanism that might allow us to know precisely why a volcano erupts." Then he added soberly, "A formidable task awaits future generations of volcanologists."

11 Kraft said those words in 1991 just before climbing Unzen, a volcano in Japan. Unzen erupted while Kraft and his wife, Katia, were on it. The couple died when a huge flood of hot gas and ash overwhelmed them.

12 Because of the guesswork involved, volcano watchers sometimes miss the mark. In 1980, they warned that Mount St. Helens might blow. They were right about the explosion. But they missed the exact time and strength of the blast. As a result, 57 people died. Still, without any kind of warning at all, as many as twenty thousand might have perished.

13 Sometimes, though, volcano watchers are impressively accurate. In 1991, they predicted the time and size of the Mount Pinatubo explosion in the Philippines. A swift evacuation saved thousands, if not tens of thousands, of lives. It is successes like this that keep volcano watchers returning to the rim of craters.

If you have been timed while reading this article, enter your reading time below. Then turn to the Words-per-Minute Table on page 71 and look up your reading speed (words per minute). Enter your reading speed on the graph on page 72.

Reading Time: Sample Lesson

________ : ________

Minutes *Seconds*

A Finding the Main Idea

One statement below expresses the main idea of the article. One statement is too general, or too broad. The other statement explains only part of the article; it is too narrow. Label the statements using the following key:

M—Main Idea **B—Too Broad** **N—Too Narrow**

N 1. As many as 27 volcano watchers have died while inspecting dangerous volcanoes in the last 50 years. [This statement is true, but it is *too narrow.* It presents only one fact from the article.]

B 2. Many professions can be quite dangerous and may even cause the death of the workers. [This statement is true, but it is *too broad.* This article is about a particular dangerous profession—volcano watching.]

M 3. Scientists who inspect volcanoes provide valuable information, but they also put themselves at risk of being killed in a sudden eruption. [This statement is the *main idea.* It tells you that the article is about scientists who study volcanoes. It also tells you why they watch volcanoes and why the job is considered risky.]

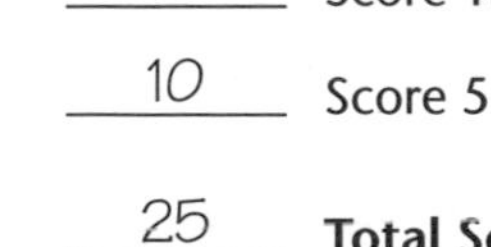

15 Score 15 points for a correct M answer.

10 Score 5 points for each correct B or N answer.

25 **Total Score:** Finding the Main Idea

B Recalling Facts

How well do you remember the facts in the article? Put an X in the box next to the answer that correctly completes each statement about the article.

1. The Galeras volcano is in
   - ☒ a. Colombia.
   - ☐ b. Japan.
   - ☐ c. Ecuador.
2. The Galeras eruption killed
   - ☒ a. six volcano watchers.
   - ☐ b. nine volcano watchers.
   - ☐ c. thousands of residents.
3. The main purpose of watching volcanoes is to
   - ☒ a. monitor them for signs of a coming eruption.
   - ☐ b. have the fun of taking a dangerous risk.
   - ☐ c. test sensitive instruments.
4. Volcano watchers Maurice and Katia Kraft died when
   - ☒ a. hot gas and ash overwhelmed them.
   - ☐ b. they were covered with molten rock.
   - ☐ c. a huge block of hot rocks struck them.
5. Volcano watchers correctly predicted the time and size of the Mount Pinatubo eruption in
   - ☐ a. Ecuador.
   - ☐ b. Japan.
   - ☒ c. the Philippines.

Score 5 points for each correct answer.

25 **Total Score:** Recalling Facts

C Making Inferences

When you combine your own experience and information from a text to draw a conclusion that is not directly stated in that text, you are making an inference. Below are five statements that may or may not be inferences based on information in the article. Label the statements using the following key:

C—Correct Inference **F—Faulty Inference**

C 1. Volcano watchers travel all around the world to inspect active volcanoes. [This is a *correct* inference. The article mentions volcano watchers at work in various locations around the globe.]

F 2. Volcano watchers enjoy the danger that is part of their profession. [This is a *faulty* inference. The article says that volcano watchers believe that the information they gather is worth the risks. It doesn't say that they enjoy the risks.]

C 3. People who live near volcanoes become used to the danger they pose. [This is a *correct* inference. The article implies that residents know that they live near volcanoes but choose to continue to live there, even though they know they must be ready to evacuate quickly.]

F 4. In the future, no one will be allowed to live near volcanoes. [This is a *faulty* inference. The article makes no mention of this.]

F 5. Only young scientists are called upon to be volcano watchers. [This is a *faulty* inference. Although some of the watchers, including the ones killed in Ecuador, are young, there is no evidence that all volcano watchers are young.]

Score 5 points for each correct answer.

25 **Total Score:** Making Inferences

D Using Words Precisely

Each numbered sentence below contains an underlined word or phrase from the article. Following the sentence are three definitions. One definition is closest to the meaning of the underlined word. One definition is opposite or nearly opposite. Label those two definitions using the following key. Do not label the remaining definition.

C—Closest **O—Opposite or Nearly Opposite**

1. None of the volcano watchers suspected that <u>molten</u> rock had pushed its way up into the volcano and was ready to erupt.

____ a. heavy
C b. melted
O c. solid

2. One block <u>nicked</u> McFarlane.

____ a. stopped
C b. wounded slightly
O c. caused serious injury to

3. They made a <u>rash</u> choice that cost them their lives.

C a. thoughtless
____ b. painful
O c. careful

4. "A <u>formidable</u> task awaits future generations of volcanologists."

C a. challenging and difficult
O b. effortless
____ c. exciting

5. Still, without any kind of warning at all, as many as twenty thousand might have perished.

O a. survived

___ b. evacuated

C c. died

15	Score 3 points for each correct C answer.
10	Score 2 points for each correct O answer.
25	**Total Score:** Using Words Precisely

Enter the four total scores in the spaces below, and add them together to find your Reading Comprehension Score. Then record your score on the graph on page 73.

Score	Question Type	Sample Lesson
25	Finding the Main Idea	
25	Recalling Facts	
25	Making Inferences	
25	Using Words Precisely	
100	**Reading Comprehension Score**	

Author's Approach

Put an X in the box next to the correct answer.

1. The main purpose of the first paragraph is to

☐ a. inform the reader about the job of a volcano watcher.

☒ b. describe the time and place of one dangerous eruption.

☐ c. explain to the reader that volcano watchers avoid risk at all times.

2. From the statements below, choose those that you believe the author would agree with.

☐ a. The decision to film the volcano in Ecuador was a sensible one, since no one could have predicted that it would ever erupt again.

☒ b. The researchers who decided to film the volcano in Ecuador did not think through their decision well enough.

☐ c. Only foolish people would ever become volcano watchers.

3. What does the author mean by the statement "Because of the guesswork involved, volcano watchers sometimes miss the mark"?

☐ a. Volcano watchers don't care if they are right or wrong.

☐ b. The predictions of volcano watchers can't be counted upon because the watchers are careless.

☒ c. Since not enough is known for sure about volcanoes, watchers sometimes guess incorrectly.

4. Choose the statement below that best describes the author's position in paragraph 13.

☐ a. Everyone was surprised when volcano watchers correctly predicted the eruption of Mount Pinatubo.

☒ b. Volcano watching is worthwhile because it saves lives.

☐ c. Scientists know enough about volcanoes.

4 Number of correct answers

Record your personal assessment of your work on the Critical Thinking Chart on page 74.

Summarizing and Paraphrasing

Put an X in the box next to the correct answer.

1. Below are summaries of the article. Choose the summary that says all the most important things about the article but in the fewest words.

☐ a. Volcano watching is dangerous, but many scientists continue to do it all over the world. [This summary leaves out almost all of the important details, such as why volcano watching is dangerous and the reasons why scientists continue to monitor volcanoes in spite of the risks.]

☐ b. Volcano watchers all over the world study volcanoes to learn more about what makes a volcano erupt. While they do their jobs, that is, monitoring volcanoes with special instruments, some of these watchers have been overwhelmed by sudden eruptions, as in Columbia, where six watchers were killed in 1993, and in Ecuador, where two researchers died later that same year. [This summary presents all of the important ideas from the article but includes too many unnecessary details.]

☒ c. Researchers who monitor volcanoes on location are often injured or even killed in sudden eruptions. They continue to risk their lives because their findings reveal much about how volcanoes work. [This summary says all the most important things about the article in the fewest words.]

2. Read the statement below about the article. Then read the paraphrase of that statement. Choose the reason that best tells why the paraphrase does not say the same thing as the statement.

Statement: The director advised the researchers to leave the area. However, they continued to stay there, either because they didn't get the message or they chose to ignore it.

Paraphrase: The researchers may have stayed in the area because they didn't get the director's message telling them to leave.

☐ a. Paraphrase says too much.

☒ b. Paraphrase doesn't say enough. [The paraphrase includes only the first possible reason why the researchers didn't follow the director's advice and ignores the second possibility—that they chose to ignore it.]

☐ c. Paraphrase doesn't agree with the statement about the article.

2 Number of correct answers

Record your personal assessment of your work on the Critical Thinking Chart on page 74.

Critical Thinking

Put an X in the box next to the correct answer for questions 1, 2, 4, and 5. Follow the directions provided for question 3.

1. Which of the following statements from the article is an opinion rather than a fact?

☒ a. "The film simply wasn't worth the risk."

☐ b. "They knew the risks involved, yet they ventured into the crater anyway."

☐ c. "The couple died when a huge flood of hot gas and ash overwhelmed them."

2. Judging by what Scott Rowland said, you can predict that he will

☒ a. continue to watch volcanoes.

☐ b. stop volcano watching because it is too dangerous.

☐ c. stop riding his bicycle to work.

3. Choose from the letters below to correctly complete the following statement. Write the letters on the lines.

On the positive side, b, but on the negative side c

a. there are volcanoes all over the world
b. volcano watchers learn much about volcanoes
c. some researchers become victims of the volcanoes

4. What was one cause of the deaths of 57 people near Mount St. Helens?

☒ a. Volcano watchers were wrong about the exact time and strength of the volcano's eruption.

☐ b. People ignored the volcano watchers' warnings.

☐ c. The volcano's eruption was totally unexpected.

5. What did you have to do to answer question 1?

☐ a. find a cause (why something happened)

☒ b. find an opinion (what someone thinks about something)

☐ c. find a reason (why something is the way it is)

5 Number of correct answers

Record your personal assessment of your work on the Critical Thinking Chart on page 74.

Personal Response

What new question do you have about this topic?

[Write any question that occurred to you as you read or as you answered the comprehension or critical thinking questions.]

Self-Assessment

Before reading this article, I already knew

[Recall the facts or concepts about volcanoes you knew before you read the article.]

Self-Assessment

To get the most out of the Critical Reading series program, you need to take charge of your own progress in improving your reading comprehension and critical thinking skills. Here are some of the features that help you work on those essential skills.

Reading Comprehension Exercises. Complete these exercises immediately after reading the article. They help you recall what you have read, understand the stated and implied main ideas, and add words to your working vocabulary.

Critical Thinking Skills Exercises. These exercises help you focus on the author's approach and purpose, recognize and generate summaries and paraphrases, and identify relationships between ideas.

Personal Response and Self-assessment. Questions in this category help you relate the articles to your personal experience and give you the opportunity to evaluate your understanding of the information in that lesson.

Compare and Contrast Charts. At the end of each unit you will complete a Compare and Contrast chart. The completed chart helps you see what the articles have in common and gives you an opportunity to explore your own ideas about the topics discussed in the articles.

The Graphs. The graphs and charts at the end of each unit enable you to keep track of your progress. Check your graphs regularly with your teacher. Decide whether your progress is satisfactory or whether you need additional work on some skills. What types of exercises are you having difficulty with? Talk with your teacher about ways to work on the skills in which you need the most practice.

UNIT ONE

MANIACS ON BIKES

Bike messengers have pretty jazzy names—Johnny Jet Fuel, Squid, Wing Nut, Mike the Bike, and Warp Drive. But the people who share city streets with them aren't impressed. Drivers, especially taxi drivers, hate these free-wheeling messengers. Pedestrians aren't too fond of them either. That's because the messengers often zip by at very high speeds just an inch or two from a bumper or a kneecap. And they do it all for the sake of delivering a package from Point A to Point B.

2 Bike messengers have been around for a long time. They go all the way back to the late 19th century in New York City and San Francisco. But they hit their heyday during the 1980s. During this decade, New York City alone had more than 5,000 bike messengers. Increased use of fax machines and e-mail has cut the number in recent years. Still, all large cities have hundreds of bike messengers whipping through the streets.

3 Bike messengers love their work. They have to. The pay is not very good. (They get paid on commission, so that the more packages they deliver, the more money

Bike messengers battle traffic, parked cars, and pedestrians as they zip through urban downtown areas delivering packages.

they earn.) Also, most bike messengers get no benefits. They get no sick leave, no paid holidays, and no health insurance. They even have to pay their own traffic tickets. On top of these drawbacks, the job is extremely dangerous. At least five riders died in New York City in 1996 alone.

4 Anyone who rides a bike on the streets of New York City probably is a bit wacky. But bike messengers are so wild that they race through the Big Apple at 25 to 30 miles per hour! They know that hair-raising speeds mean more money, and so they don't let the rules of the road slow them down. Red lights only cost time and money, so bike messengers routinely ignore them. If going the wrong way down a one-way street saves time, the messengers do it. Hopping curbs and riding on the sidewalk is fair game. So, too, is biking up or down a set of stairs. The trick is to dodge all the cars and people and deliver the package on time. One messenger, called Steve the Greek, compares blasting through New York City traffic on a bike to "skiing on a mountain that moves."

5 Many bike messengers think of themselves as rebels. They go out of their way to express their individuality. Some dye their hair purple or green. Many sport nose rings, tongue studs, and tattoos. Some riders shave their heads while others wear ponytails or dreadlocks.

6 Bike messengers are mostly in their 20s and in terrific shape. There is no sex discrimination in this business. Although most of the riders are men, there are plenty of women messengers. And they are just as crazy as the men. "I love the adrenaline rush that comes from being scared," says Pixie Marquis.

7 Naturally, all riders love to bike. Also, they crave the freedom the job provides. Stepha, a woman rider, says, "We know how free it is to have a job without walls. And of course we're completely in love with riding our bicycles." Most riders have little respect for people who sit behind the wheel of a car. Says Stepha, "We don't understand why everyone in the world doesn't bike."

8 Fellow bikers are the only ones who really understand what the job is like. So bikers tend to hang out together after hours to share war stories and close

A New York City bike messenger has a risky job.

encounters. They have even created their own special jargon. *Shooting the tube*, for example, means "squeezing between two city buses." *Blowing lights* means "to run through a set of red lights." A *copsicle* is a policeman on a bike. And an *urban log food* is a burrito.

9 Bike messengers ride tough old bikes with fat tires. To deter thieves, they often paint their bikes some hideous color. Most of the riders prefer low-tech equipment. Many bikes, for instance, have just one gear. "To be a bike courier," says one rider, "is to be able to ride through rain, snow and mud—it's not about having the hottest stuff and strutting it around."

10 Some riders have turned their job into a competitive sport. They now have their own Cycle Messenger World Championship. Each year the competition is held in a different country. The games draw hundreds of riders from around the world. Bicyclists race through a course that resembles their daily runs. They must deliver a certain number of packages to a set number of destinations.

11 The World Championships, however, are too big to be a real test. With so many riders, the police have to close off the streets. To some purists, there's no fun without the potentially deadly traffic. "If they really wanted to make the race authentic," says one rider, "they'd have us run through traffic while people opened car doors."

12 Some competitions come close to that standard. In New York City, bike messengers put on a Halloween race each year. It is held during the height of rush-hour traffic. Competitors have to dodge the cars *and* the police. For many riders, this Halloween race is the ultimate challenge. As one racer, known as Squid, says, "You're racing people, but you're also racing against the city." In 1996, John Yacobellis, the race winner, "caught a ride." While on the West Side Highway, he grabbed hold of a speeding car. But since this race has no rules, that tactic wasn't considered cheating.

13 The best maniacs on bikes are incredibly good. They can cover 15 miles in less than an hour during rush-hour traffic, stopping six times. For them, such records are not only badges of pride, but also a measure of how much fun they're having. "I was thinking about medical school," says messenger Adam Ford. "But [biking] is just so much more entertaining. Why would I want to forfeit my youth to go to medical school?"

If you have been timed while reading this article, enter your reading time below. Then turn to the Words-per-Minute Table on page 71 and look up your reading speed (words per minute). Enter your reading speed on the graph on page 72.

Reading Time: Lesson 1

_______ : _______

Minutes *Seconds*

A Finding the Main Idea

One statement below expresses the main idea of the article. One statement is too general, or too broad. The other statement explains only part of the article; it is too narrow. Label the statements using the following key:

M—Main Idea **B—Too Broad** **N—Too Narrow**

_______ 1. City streets with heavy traffic present a challenge to travelers who need to get from Point A to Point B.

_______ 2. Bike messengers enjoy the challenge and the danger involved in delivering mail around big cities.

_______ 3. Because bike messengers often choose to ignore the rules of the road, they are not popular with taxi drivers or pedestrians.

_______ Score 15 points for a correct M answer.

_______ Score 5 points for each correct B or N answer.

_______ **Total Score:** Finding the Main Idea

Recalling Facts

How well do you remember the facts in the article? Put an X in the box next to the answer that correctly completes each statement about the article.

1. Bike messengers were most common during the
- ☐ a. 1980s.
- ☐ b. 1890s.
- ☐ c. 1970s.

2. Bike messengers are paid
- ☐ a. a set salary, no matter how many packages they deliver.
- ☐ b. about $4.00 per hour.
- ☐ c. for every package they deliver.

3. The phrase *shooting the tube* means
- ☐ a. "going the wrong way down a one-way street."
- ☐ b. "squeezing between two buses."
- ☐ c. "running a red light."

4. The Cycle Messenger World Championship is held in
- ☐ a. a different country each year.
- ☐ b. New York City.
- ☐ c. San Francisco.

5. The Halloween race held in New York City each year takes place
- ☐ a. at midnight.
- ☐ b. during rush hour.
- ☐ c. at sunrise

Score 5 points for each correct answer.

_______ **Total Score:** Recalling Facts

C Making Inferences

When you combine your own experience and information from a text to draw a conclusion that is not directly stated in that text, you are making an inference. Below are five statements that may or may not be inferences based on information in the article. Label the statements using the following key:

C—Correct Inference **F—Faulty Inference**

_______ 1. City police ignore traffic violations when they see that bike messengers are in a hurry.

_______ 2. Most bike messengers dream of owning a fancy car someday.

_______ 3. To stay safe, people walking in New York City should keep an eye out for bike messengers.

_______ 4. Most bike messengers spend a great deal of money on their bikes.

_______ 5. Bike messengers have quick reflexes and good coordination.

Score 5 points for each correct answer.

_______ **Total Score:** Making Inferences

D Using Words Precisely

Each numbered sentence below contains an underlined word or phrase from the article. Following the sentence are three definitions. One definition is closest to the meaning of the underlined word. One definition is opposite or nearly opposite. Label those two definitions using the following key. Do not label the remaining definition.

C—Closest **O—Opposite or Nearly Opposite**

1. Drivers, especially taxi drivers, hate these freewheeling messengers.

_______ a. uptight

_______ b. not bound by rules

_______ c. fast-moving

2. Red lights only cost time and money, so bike messengers routinely ignore them.

_______ a. happily

_______ b. seldom

_______ c. regularly

3. Also, they crave the freedom the job provides.

_______ a. desire or need intensely

_______ b. advertise

_______ c. are indifferent about

4. For many riders, this Halloween race is the ultimate challenge.

_______ a. smallest

_______ b. most extreme

_______ c. current

5. "Why would I want to forfeit my youth to go to medical school?"

_______ a. gain

_______ b. sacrifice

_______ c. celebrate

_______ Score 3 points for each correct C answer.

_______ Score 2 points for each correct O answer.

_______ **Total Score:** Using Words Precisely

Enter the four total scores in the spaces below, and add them together to find your Reading Cómprehension Score. Then record your score on the graph on page 73.

Score	Question Type	Lesson 1
_______	Finding the Main Idea	
_______	Recalling Facts	
_______	Making Inferences	
_______	Using Words Precisely	
_______	**Reading Comprehension Score**	

Author's Approach

Put an X in the box next to the correct answer.

1. The author uses the first sentence of the article to

☐ a. inform the reader about the dangers of being a bike messenger.

☐ b. explain the bike messenger's job to the reader.

☐ c. create a light, informal mood.

2. What does the author mean by the statement "Bike messengers love their work. They have to"?

☐ a. Being a bike messenger has many drawbacks, therefore those who make it their career must do it just for fun.

☐ b. Bike messengers must love their work because no one loves them.

☐ c. The only place where bike messengers can be happy is on the job.

3. From the statements below, choose those that you believe the author would agree with.

☐ a. Bike messengers are different in many ways from those whose lives are spent in traditional jobs.

☐ b. Bike messengers should adopt a more traditional way of dressing so they can look more businesslike.

☐ c. Bike messengers are proud of their physical ability and their riding skill.

_______ Number of correct answers

Record your personal assessment of your work on the Critical Thinking Chart on page 74.

Summarizing and Paraphrasing

Follow the directions provided for question 1. Put an X in the box next to the correct answer for the other questions.

1. Reread paragraph 9 in the article. Below, write a summary of the paragraph in no more than 25 words.

____

____

____

____

Reread your summary and decide whether it covers the important ideas in the paragraph. Next, decide how to shorten the summary to 15 words or less without leaving out any essential information. Write this summary below.

____

____

____

2. Read the statement below about the article. Then read the paraphrase of that statement. Choose the reason that best tells why the paraphrase does not say the same thing as the statement.

   Statement: Bike messengers are not paid well and they don't get the benefits that most people expect from a job.

   Paraphrase: Bike messengers don't care that they will never earn much money or receive benefits.

☐ a. Paraphrase says too much.
☐ b. Paraphrase doesn't say enough.
☐ c. Paraphrase doesn't agree with the statement about the article.

3. Choose the sentence that correctly restates the following sentence from the article:

   "To deter thieves, they often paint their bikes some hideous color."

☐ a. To make their bikes less obvious to thieves, bike messengers often paint them dull colors.
☐ b. Bike messengers sometimes paint their bikes ugly colors in order to discourage thieves from stealing them.
☐ c. Bike messengers know that thieves are looking only for bikes that are painted beautifully, so they paint theirs with dark colors.

_______ Number of correct answers

Record your personal assessment of your work on the Critical Thinking Chart on page 74.

Critical Thinking

Put an X in the box next to the correct answer for questions 1 and 2. Follow the directions provided for questions 3 and 4.

1. Which of the following statements from the article is an opinion rather than a fact?

☐ a. "Bike messengers ride tough old bikes with fat tires."
☐ b. "At least five riders died in New York City in 1996 alone."
☐ c. "Anyone who rides a bike on the street of New York City probably is a bit wacky."

2. From what the article told about the effect that faxes and e-mail have had on the number of bike messengers, you can predict that as computers become more common, bike messengers will

☐ a. disappear altogether.

☐ b. decrease in number.

☐ c. increase in number.

3. Choose from the letters below to correctly complete the following statement. Write the letters on the lines.

   On the positive side, ________, but on the negative side ________.

   a. bike messengers take unnecessary risks
   b. bike messengers have a lot of fun
   c. bike messengers have created their own jargon

4. Read paragraph 2. Then choose from the letters below to correctly complete the following statement. Write the letters on the lines.

   According to paragraph 2, ________ because ________.

   a. the number of bike messengers has decreased
   b. bike messengers have been around for many years
   c. people are using more faxes and e-mail to send messages

________ Number of correct answers

Record your personal assessment of your work on the Critical Thinking Chart on page 74.

Personal Response

Would you recommend this article to other students? Explain.

____

____

____

____

Self-Assessment

One of the things I did best when reading this article was

____

____

____

____

I believe I did this well because

____

____

____

____

"QUEEN BESS" COLEMAN

Bessie Coleman's brother was just having a little fun. Newly returned from military service in France during World War I, he kidded his sister about French women. Unlike Bessie, he said, they were free to do anything they wanted. They could have their own careers. They could even fly their own planes.

2 Bessie's brother knew that Bessie dreamed of being a pilot. She had read all the accounts of pilot exploits in the war. But she faced two barriers. First, she was a woman, and women were not supposed to become pilots. And second, she was an African American. What white male pilot would teach a black woman to fly in 1919? The answer was no one.

3 That didn't stop Bessie Coleman. She had overcome tough times in the past. Born in 1892 to a dirt-poor family in Texas, she had little schooling. As soon as she was old enough, she had been expected to pick cotton to help her family survive. But Bessie loved books and read as many as she could. Reading helped open her eyes to the wider world and, in

Flying circuses were popular in the early part of the century, and wing-walking was a popular stunt. Some people, such as the woman in this photo, performed stunts such as these to pay for flying lessons.

1915, she moved to Chicago. The city offered her far more opportunities than her small Texas town. Before long, she had found work as a manicurist. She was so good she won a contest as the best black manicurist in Chicago.

4 It was her brother's tales of French life that changed Bessie's life. His teasing had a positive side. Bessie learned that not only were French women free to do as they pleased, but there was no prejudice against blacks in France. If Bessie really wanted to fly, she decided, she would have to go to France to do it. So Bessie worked even harder to earn the money she needed for the trip. She also began to study French.

5 In 1920, Bessie set sail for France. She was readily accepted into a topflight program. Seven months later she became the first black woman to earn a pilot's license. A year later, she sailed back to the United States. She now looked the part of a dashing aviator. She wore a tailored flying suit and a leather coat. The African-American press welcomed her, dubbing her "Queen Bess." The white press, on the other hand, ignored her.

6 Flying was so new at this time that "air shows" were a major attraction. Pilots "barnstormed" from town to town, dazzling fans with their stunt flying. They did loop-the-loops, figure eights, and other daring stunts. Once again, Bessie ran into the racism of her day. No white pilots would teach her these aerobatics. In 1922, she returned to France to learn these skills.

7 In France, films were made of Bessie's stunt flying. When these films were shown in the United States, Bessie became a hot news item. Even the white press covered her return home. Soon Bessie was touring the country, amazing everyone with her flying skills. She did all the crazy loops and dives that male pilots did. Crowds of 10,000 fans or more often

Bessie Coleman, the first African-American woman to earn a pilot's license, receives a bouquet from aeronautical instructor Captain Edison C. McEvy.

showed up to see her and other pilots defy gravity.

8 "Queen Bess" used her fame to fight racism. She refused to perform in any air show that did not let African Americans attend. She gave lectures to black churches and community groups about the future of aviation. She also talked to children in black schools. Her ultimate goal was to open her own school to train black pilots. Running a school would cost a lot of money, so Bessie planned to keep performing and lecturing until she had saved enough.

9 Stunt flying, of course, was a risky business. Early planes were flimsy and their engines unreliable. All kinds of pilots, not just stunt pilots, crashed. One day, in 1923, Bessie ran into trouble while flying to an air show in California. She had just taken off when her engine stalled. The plane plunged 300 feet and crashed. Bessie was lucky to survive. But she had suffered a broken leg, fractured ribs, and many cuts and bruises.

10 It took Bess three months to recover her health. The plane, which she had recently purchased, was a total loss. So Bessie decided to take "a good long rest." By 1925, however, she was barnstorming once again, this time with a new plane. In an effort to please her fans with even more daring stunts, Bessie added parachute jumping to her act. With the money she was making, it seemed her dream of opening her own school for black pilots would soon come true.

11 On May 1, 1926, Bessie was scheduled to give an air show at Paxon Field in Jacksonville, Florida. On the day before the show, she wanted to check out the field. She planned to parachute and needed a good landing site. So she asked William Wills, her mechanic, to take her up in the plane. She wanted him to do the flying so she would be free to look over the side of the plane.

12 Bessie jumped into the rear cockpit. For some reason, she didn't fasten her seatbelt. Perhaps she just wanted to be able to lean further out over the side. Wills climbed a few thousand feet and then circled around to return to Paxon Field.

13 Witnesses later said they saw the plane go into a tailspin at about 1,000 feet. The plane flipped upside down at 500 feet, tossing Bessie out. The fall, which broke nearly every bone in her body, killed her instantly. She was 34 years old.

14 Wills failed to regain control of the plane and he, too, died. The cause of the tailspin was quickly discovered. A mechanic's wrench had slid into the control gears, jamming them.

15 "Queen Bess" Coleman was buried in Chicago. In her honor, flying clubs named Bessie Coleman Aero Groups were organized. These clubs sponsored the first all-black air show in 1931. A flying school for African Americans was opened a year later. In Chicago, a street and a library are named after Bess Coleman. Her face has also appeared on U.S. postage stamps. And every year, fellow pilots fly over her grave and remember Bess's amazing perseverance, skill, and daring.

If you have been timed while reading this article, enter your reading time below. Then turn to the Words-per-Minute Table on page 71 and look up your reading speed (words per minute). Enter your reading speed on the graph on page 72.

Reading Time: Lesson 2

_______ : _______

Minutes *Seconds*

 A Finding the Main Idea

One statement below expresses the main idea of the article. One statement is too general, or too broad. The other statement explains only part of the article; it is too narrow. Label the statements using the following key:

M—Main Idea **B—Too Broad** **N—Too Narrow**

______ 1. Bess Coleman refused to let racism stop her from becoming a popular stunt pilot during the 1920s.

______ 2. To learn to fly, stunt pilot Bess Coleman had to travel to France in 1920.

______ 3. Stunt flying during the 1920s demanded extraordinary skill and daring.

______ Score 15 points for a correct M answer.

______ Score 5 points for each correct B or N answer.

______ **Total Score:** Finding the Main Idea

 B Recalling Facts

How well do you remember the facts in the article? Put an X in the box next to the answer that correctly completes each statement about the article.

1. Bessie Coleman was born in
   - ☐ a. France.
   - ☐ b. Texas.
   - ☐ c. Chicago.
2. African-American reporters named Bessie
   - ☐ a. Queen Bess.
   - ☐ b. Barnstorming Bessie.
   - ☐ c. the Flying Manicurist.
3. Bessie planned to perform until she had enough money to
   - ☐ a. retire to France.
   - ☐ b. open a school for black pilots.
   - ☐ c. build a library in Chicago.
4. On the day she died, Bessie was not flying the plane because she
   - ☐ a. wanted to look for a good spot to land her parachute.
   - ☐ b. didn't feel well.
   - ☐ c. was teaching the pilot how to fly.
5. Bess died near an airfield in
   - ☐ a. California.
   - ☐ b. Chicago.
   - ☐ c. Jacksonville, Florida.

Score 5 points for each correct answer.

______ **Total Score:** Recalling Facts

C Making Inferences

When you combine your own experience and information from a text to draw a conclusion that is not directly stated in that text, you are making an inference. Below are five statements that may or may not be inferences based on information in the article. Label the statements using the following key:

C—Correct Inference **F—Faulty Inference**

_______ 1. All the women in France had careers in the years following World War I.

_______ 2. Bessie Coleman was an especially determined and persistent person.

_______ 3. Bessie was often the only female pilot performing in an air show.

_______ 4. During the 1920s, African Americans were not always allowed to attend air shows.

_______ 5. William Wills, Bess's mechanic who piloted her final flight, had never flown a plane before that fateful day.

Score 5 points for each correct answer.

_______ **Total Score:** Making Inferences

D Using Words Precisely

Each numbered sentence below contains an underlined word or phrase from the article. Following the sentence are three definitions. One definition is closest to the meaning of the underlined word. One definition is opposite or nearly opposite. Label those two definitions using the following key. Do not label the remaining definition.

C—Closest **O—Opposite or Nearly Opposite**

1. She was readily accepted into a topflight program.

_______ a. substandard

_______ b. difficult

_______ c. excellent

2. She now looked the part of a dashing aviator.

_______ a. foreign

_______ b. stylish

_______ c. dowdy

3. Pilots "barnstormed" from town to town, dazzling fans with their stunt flying.

_______ a. impressing

_______ b. disappointing

_______ c. applauding

4. Early planes were flimsy and their engines unreliable.

_______ a. strong and well-made

_______ b. expensive

_______ c. fragile

5. The fall, which broke nearly every bone in her body, killed her instantly.

_______ a. immediately

_______ b. eventually

_______ c. thoughtlessly

_______ Score 3 points for each correct C answer.

_______ Score 2 points for each correct O answer.

_______ **Total Score:** Using Words Precisely

Enter the four total scores in the spaces below, and add them together to find your Reading Comprehension Score. Then record your score on the graph on page 73.

Score	Question Type	Lesson 2
_______	Finding the Main Idea	
_______	Recalling Facts	
_______	Making Inferences	
_______	Using Words Precisely	
_______	**Reading Comprehension Score**	

Author's Approach

Put an X in the box next to the correct answer.

1. What is the author's purpose in writing "'Queen Bess' Coleman"?

☐ a. To encourage the reader to become a stunt pilot

☐ b. To inform the reader about a courageous woman's life

☐ c. To convey a mood of fear and danger

2. In this article, the statement "The white press, on the other hand, ignored her" means

☐ a. white reporters knew nothing about Bess.

☐ b. Bess was not interested in speaking to white reporters, so they ignored her.

☐ c. Bess was a victim of racial prejudice just because she was an African American.

3. How is the author's purpose for writing the article expressed in paragraph 8?

☐ a. The paragraph describes the way Bess fought back against racism and planned to use her skills to help other black pilots.

☐ b. The paragraph explains that Bess needed a lot of money.

☐ c. The paragraph describes the way Bess lectured about the future of aviation.

4. The author tells this story mainly by

☐ a. retelling personal experiences.

☐ b. comparing different topics.

☐ c. relating events in the order they happened.

_______ Number of correct answers

Record your personal assessment of your work on the Critical Thinking Chart on page 74.

Summarizing and Paraphrasing

Follow the directions provided for questions 1 and 2. Put an X in the box next to the correct answer for question 3.

1. Look for the important ideas and events in paragraphs 4 and 5. Summarize those paragraphs in one or two sentences.

____

____

____

2. Complete the following one-sentence summary of the article using the lettered phrases from the phrase bank below. Write the letters on the lines.

Phrase Bank:

a. how Bess became a famous pilot
b. Bessie's brother's teasing
c. Bess's death and the ways people have honored her

The article about Bess Coleman begins with________, goes on to explain________, and ends with________.

3. Choose the sentence that correctly restates the following sentence from the article:

"In an effort to please her fans with even more daring stunts, Bessie added parachute jumping to her act."

☐ a. Bessie learned how to parachute jump because she was losing her fans.

☐ b. Because her fans wanted to see more daring stunts, Bessie began to parachute jump as part of her act.

☐ c. Although Bessie preferred stunt flying, her fans told her to add parachute jumping to her act.

________ Number of correct answers

Record your personal assessment of your work on the Critical Thinking Chart on page 74.

Critical Thinking

Follow the directions provided for questions 1 and 3. Put an X in the box next to the correct answer for the other questions.

1. For each statement below, write O if it expresses an opinion or write F if it expresses a fact.

_______ a. Films showing Bess's stunt flying skills were shown in the U.S.

_______ b. It was foolhardy of Bess to continue flying even after her plane crashed in 1923.

_______ c. Pilots in the 1920s were more skillful than pilots are today.

2. Considering Bess Coleman's actions as described in this article, you can predict that if she had lived, she would have

- ☐ a. saved enough money to begin her own school for black pilots in the U.S.
- ☐ b. decided that fighting racism was too difficult and moved to France.
- ☐ c. begun a school for only black women pilots in France.

3. Choose from the letters below to correctly complete the following statement. Write the letters on the lines.

In the article, ________ and ________ were different.

- a. opportunities for African Americans in France during the 1920s
- b. opportunities for African Americans in the United States during the 1920s
- c. opportunities for African Americans in England during the 1920s

4. What was the effect of the mechanic's wrench sliding into the control gears on Bess's plane?

- ☐ a. The plane circled Paxon Field.
- ☐ b. The engine stalled.
- ☐ c. The pilot lost control and the plane crashed.

5. What did you have to do to answer question 3?

- ☐ a. find a contrast (how things are different)
- ☐ b. find a purpose (why something is done)
- ☐ c. draw a conclusion (a sensible statement based on the text and your experience)

________ Number of correct answers

Record your personal assessment of your work on the Critical Thinking Chart on page 74.

Personal Response

How do you think Bessie felt when her brother told her about the opportunities for women in France?

____

____

____

____

Self-Assessment

From reading this article, I have learned

____

____

____

____

JACKIE CHAN
Actor and Stuntman

Actor and stuntman Jackie Chan performs a stunt in the film Rumble in the Bronx.

"I do a lot of things that normal people can't do," says Jackie Chan.

2 That's putting it mildly. Chan does things so extreme they have to be seen to be believed. And what you see in a Jackie Chan film is the real thing. Chan refuses to use doubles or stuntmen or tricky camera angles.

3 Some of the stunts he does are pretty incredible. Take, for example, one scene in *Police Story II*. Chan needs to get from one side of the street to the other. Most people would go to the corner, wait for the traffic light to change, and walk across the street. That's not Chan's style. Instead, he jumps off a balcony onto a truck going in one direction. He then leaps to the roof of a double-decker bus going the other way. Finally, he jumps through a second-floor window to catch up to the bad guy.

4 While filming *Rumble in the Bronx*, Chan jumped off a tall bridge onto a moving hovercraft. The force of the landing broke his ankle. Yet with the cameras still rolling, he somehow managed to barefoot ski behind the hovercraft. In *Police Story III*, Chan hangs

from a helicopter on a rope ladder. He gets slammed into walls, billboards, and a moving train. In *Project A*, Chan gets handcuffed to a flag pole. He escapes by climbing up the pole and jumping off the top. In the same movie he falls three stories through two awnings and lands on the hard ground. Chan did this stunt three times to get it just right.

5 Chan has bounced down a hill inside a giant beach ball. He has leaped off a mountaintop onto a passing hot air balloon. And he has caught a ride on a speeding bus by hooking an umbrella handle onto a window ledge. Even when he *could* fake stunts, he doesn't. He really has run across flaming coals. He really has swallowed industrial strength alcohol and a handful of red-hot chili peppers.

6 If you still don't believe what you see in his movies, watch the credits at the end. They show the outtakes—scenes of stunts that went wrong or were not used in the film. Sometimes they show the missed stunts from different angles. What other action hero in the movies shows you his mistakes?

7 Not surprisingly, Chan gets hurt every now and then. But he takes a certain pride in all his broken bones. What exactly has he broken? As he describes it: "My skull, my eyes, my nose three times, my jaw, my shoulder, my chest, two fingers, a knee—everything from the top of my head to the bottom of my feet."

8 One of Chan's stunts nearly got him killed. In *The Armor of God*, he made what for him was a fairly routine jump off a castle wall. But he missed the tree branch he was supposed to catch and fell 40 feet. Chan hit a rock, splitting open the right side of his head. He later recuperated from the injury and now enjoys showing off the hole in his head. He even lets a few people stick their finger in it. Why does he do such loony stunts? "As long as the camera is rolling," he says, "I'll just do it."

9 And the cameras have been rolling for Chan since 1976. Over the years, he has made more than 40 films. He began his career doing stunts for other people, but was so good that he quickly began to star in his own movies. At first, movie directors thought Chan might be the second Bruce Lee. (At the time, Lee was the most famous action hero in Asia.) But Chan soon found his own style. He blended sparkling comedy with exciting kung fu action. "When Bruce Lee punched someone, he kept going like it didn't hurt," Chan says. "I shake my hand and go, 'Ow!'" Movie fans wince *and* laugh when they see Jackie Chan in action.

10 Chan's first major movie was *Snake in the Eagle's Shadow*. Filmed in 1978, it broke all box office records in Asia at that time. Chan's second movie, *Drunken Master*, did even better. At that point,

A poster advertises the Jackie Chan film Operation Condor.

Chan could do anything he wanted to do. He began directing his own films and choreographing his own stunts. He even began to sing the title song in some of his movies. Jackie Chan became, perhaps, the world's best-loved movie star. He certainly holds that title in Asia. As he once said, "In Asia, I am *Jurassic Park*. I am *E.T.*"

11 Where did Chan develop such talents? He grew up in Hong Kong. At the age of 7, his parents sent him to study at the Chinese Opera Institute. Opera in China is different from opera in the rest of the world. It is more than music; it is a form of military training. Chan studied 19 hours a day. His day began at 5 A.M. and didn't end until midnight. During that time, Chan studied dance, song, acrobatics, and kung fu.

12 The training was brutal. The instructor's stick was never very far away. "I was beaten every day," Chan remembers. "I was very angry." There was only one way to avoid a beating—and that was to do what the teacher demanded. "I had to learn everything—jumping, punching, kicking," he remembers. "I didn't want to learn it, but the teacher's stick forced me to learn it. If I said I couldn't jump, the teacher would stand up and I'd jump 10 feet."

13 Chan spent 10 years at the Institute. The cruel training paid off. When he left at the age of 17, he wasn't afraid of anything. His teachers had made him fearless. But courage alone would have made him only a great stuntman. Jackie Chan is much more than that. True, no other action hero comes close to matching his stunts. But Jackie Chan has combined his many talents with a sense of humor and has, in the process, turned himself into a star.

If you have been timed while reading this article, enter your reading time below. Then turn to the Words-per-Minute Table on page 71 and look up your reading speed (words per minute). Enter your reading speed on the graph on page 72.

Reading Time: Lesson 3

________ : ________

Minutes *Seconds*

A Finding the Main Idea

One statement below expresses the main idea of the article. One statement is too general, or too broad. The other statement explains only part of the article; it is too narrow. Label the statements using the following key:

M—Main Idea **B—Too Broad** **N—Too Narrow**

_____ 1. Movie star Jackie Chan fearlessly does all his own movie stunts and combines skill with a sense of humor.

_____ 2. To prepare for his career in movies, Jackie Chan completed rigorous training at the Chinese Opera Institute.

_____ 3. Jackie Chan doesn't let a little danger stop him from entertaining people all over the world.

_____ Score 15 points for a correct M answer.

_____ Score 5 points for each correct B or N answer.

_____ **Total Score:** Finding the Main Idea

B Recalling Facts

How well do you remember the facts in the article? Put an X in the box next to the answer that correctly completes each statement about the article.

1. After Jackie Chan broke his ankle while making a film, he
- ☐ a. demanded that the film be shot again.
- ☐ b. skied barefoot.
- ☐ c. sued the movie studio for unsafe working conditions.

2. According to the article, Jackie Chan has performed all these stunts except
- ☐ a. falling from the Empire State Building.
- ☐ b. bouncing downhill inside a beach ball.
- ☐ c. running across flaming coals.

3. Chan's first major movie role was in
- ☐ a. *Police Story II.*
- ☐ b. *Rumble in the Bronx.*
- ☐ c. *Snake in the Eagle's Shadow.*

4. At the Chinese Opera Institute, Chan's training began each day at
- ☐ a. 5 A.M.
- ☐ b. 9 A.M.
- ☐ c. midnight.

5. At the end of Jackie Chan movies, audiences see
- ☐ a. other stuntmen trying Chan's stunts.
- ☐ b. pictures of Chan as a boy at the Institute.
- ☐ c. unused movie clips of stunts that went wrong.

Score 5 points for each correct answer.

_____ **Total Score:** Recalling Facts

C Making Inferences

When you combine your own experience and information from a text to draw a conclusion that is not directly stated in that text, you are making an inference. Below are five statements that may or may not be inferences based on information in the article. Label the statements using the following key:

C—Correct Inference **F—Faulty Inference**

_______ 1. No other movie stars do their own stunts in action films.

_______ 2. Jackie Chan is always sure that he can perform each stunt perfectly before he tries it.

_______ 3. If you can do your own stunts, you are almost certain to be a star.

_______ 4. Jackie Chan works hard at his job.

_______ 5. When a stuntman performs a trick, several cameras film his performance.

Score 5 points for each correct answer.

_______ **Total Score:** Making Inferences

D Using Words Precisely

Each numbered sentence below contains an underlined word or phrase from the article. Following the sentence are three definitions. One definition is closest to the meaning of the underlined word. One definition is opposite or nearly opposite. Label those two definitions using the following key. Do not label the remaining definition.

C—Closest **O—Opposite or Nearly Opposite**

1. In *The Armor of God*, he made what for him was a fairly routine jump off a castle wall.

_______ a. extraordinary

_______ b. everyday

_______ c. exciting

2. He later recuperated from the injury and now enjoys showing off the hole in his head.

_______ a. suffered again

_______ b. recovered

_______ c. worsened

3. Why does he do such loony stunts?

_______ a. sensible

_______ b. fabulous

_______ c. foolish

4. It is more than music: it is a form of military training.

_______ a. relating to civilians and peace

_______ b. relating to soldiers or war

_______ c. relating to music and dance

5. The training was brutal.

_______ a. old-fashioned

_______ b. harsh

_______ c. kind

_______ Score 3 points for each correct C answer.

_______ Score 2 points for each correct O answer.

_______ **Total Score:** Using Words Precisely

Enter the four total scores in the spaces below, and add them together to find your Reading Comprehension Score. Then record your score on the graph on page 73.

Score	Question Type	Lesson 3
_______	Finding the Main Idea	
_______	Recalling Facts	
_______	Making Inferences	
_______	Using Words Precisely	
_______	**Reading Comprehension Score**	

Author's Approach

Put an X in the box next to the correct answer.

1. The author uses the first sentence of the article to

☐ a. introduce the reader to what's special about Jackie Chan.

☐ b. compare Jackie Chan with other stuntmen.

☐ c. entertain the reader with a funny story about Jackie Chan.

2. What does the author mean by the statement "And what you see in a Jackie Chan film is the real thing"?

☐ a. Jackie Chan always plays himself in his movies.

☐ b. Jackie Chan never fakes his stunts or has a professional stuntman fill in for him.

☐ c. Jackie Chan is a real person.

3. From the statements below, choose those that you believe the author would agree with.

☐ a. Jackie Chan is a highly skilled and inventive athlete and actor.

☐ b. Jackie Chan deserves the fame he has achieved.

☐ c. Films featuring Jackie Chan are known mostly for their complex stories and their well-developed characters.

4. In this article, "In Asia, I [Jackie Chan] am *Jurassic Park*. I am *E.T.*" means

☐ a. Jackie Chan feels that he is extremely popular in Asia.

☐ b. Jackie Chan would like to make a movie in Asia that is as popular as *Jurassic Park* and *E.T.* were in the United States.

☐ c. Jackie Chan is afraid that people in Asia confuse his films with other American films such as *Jurassic Park* or *E.T.*

_______ Number of correct answers

Record your personal assessment of your work on the Critical Thinking Chart on page 74.

Summarizing and Paraphrasing

Put an X in the box next to the correct answer.

1. Below are summaries of the article. Choose the summary that says all the most important things about the article but in the fewest words.

☐ a. Although Jackie Chan was first expected to be a second Bruce Lee, his personal style emerged and made him a star in his own right.

☐ b. Movie star Jackie Chan has done incredible stunts such as jumping off buildings into moving vehicles, leaping off tall bridges, climbing up poles and jumping off them, and catching a ride on a speeding bus.

☐ c. Movie star Jackie Chan does amazing stunts and blends them with a pleasing sense of humor. Tough training he endured as a child developed his physical skills enough to make the stunts look easy and fun.

2. Choose the best one-sentence paraphrase for the following sentence from the article:

"He [Chan] began his career doing stunts for other people, but was so good that he quickly began to star in his own movies."

☐ a. Early in his career, Chan did other stars' stunts, but when people noticed how skillful he was, he was given starring roles himself.

☐ b. Other stars asked that Chan do their stunts, but he was destined to be a star himself.

☐ c. When he was young, Chan did other people's stunts, but then he began to make up stunts of his own.

_________ Number of correct answers

Record your personal assessment of your work on the Critical Thinking Chart on page 74.

Critical Thinking

Put an X in the box next to the correct answer for questions 1, 2, 4, and 5. Follow the directions provided for question 3.

1. Which of the following statements from the article is an opinion rather than a fact?

☐ a. "Over the years, he has made more than 40 films."

☐ b. "Some of the stunts he does are pretty incredible."

☐ c. "Filmed in 1978, it broke all box office records in Asia at that time."

2. From what Jackie Chan said, you can predict that if he is hired to do other films, he will probably

☐ a. direct other actors but not appear in the film himself.

☐ b. refuse to do any more of his own stunts.

☐ c. continue to try difficult stunts.

3. Choose from the letters below to correctly complete the following statement. Write the letters on the lines.

According to the article, _________ caused Jackie Chan to _________, and the effect was _________.

a. become fearless

b. brutal training Chan went through as a child

c. Chan became a great stuntman

4. How is Jackie Chan an example of a daredevil?

☐ a. He has become an international movie star.

☐ b. He is sometimes in dangerous situations.

☐ c. He chooses to engage in activities that could injure or even kill him.

5. What did you have to do to answer question 1?

- ☐ a. find an opinion (what someone thinks about something)
- ☐ b. find a cause (why something happened)
- ☐ c. draw a conclusion (a sensible statement based on the text and your experience)

_________ Number of correct answers

Record your personal assessment of your work on the Critical Thinking Chart on page 74.

Personal Response

A question I would like answered by Jackie Chan is

____

____

____

____

Self-Assessment

The part I found most difficult about the article was

____

____

____

____

I found this difficult because

____

____

____

____

RODEO CLOWNS

Rodeo clowns are often called bullfighters. But they have little in common with Spanish matadors. Rodeo clowns have no red capes or sequined vests or swords. And rodeo bulls always live to fight another day. They don't end up like Spanish bulls—dead, with their bodies stuck like pincushions. If anyone is going to get killed in the rodeo, it won't be the bull—it will be the rodeo clown.

2 With the rest of the crowd, these clowns watch as a rodeo rider climbs onto a bull. The rider tries to stay on the wildly bucking bull for eight seconds. If the rider succeeds, he then quickly jumps off the animal. Often, though, the bull tosses the rider before the eight-second horn goes off. Either way, the rider ends up on the ground along with a 1,500-pound bull who is looking for someone to hurt. That's when rodeo clowns spring into action.

3 Somehow the clowns must distract the bull so the rider can run to the fence and climb to safety. The clowns will taunt the bull. They might wave a towel or a rag at him to get him to charge. Then, at the last second, the clowns dodge the charging bull and skip away. Lecile Harris, a retired

A rodeo clown performs for the crowd at a rodeo in Salinas, California.

rodeo clown, always enjoyed the thrill of taunting and dodging an angry bull. "I really loved to fight bulls," Harris recalled. "To move in on a bull, to touch his face, his head, and get out again—that's like hitting a home run for me."

4 Touching any bull in the face is asking for trouble. Bulls are fiercely territorial creatures. They feel the ring belongs to them. They don't treat trespassers lightly. Unlike horses, who kick riders only by accident, bulls sometimes go out of their way to hurt people. These agile animals will stomp a fallen rider and try to gore him with their horns. The job of the clown is to jump between the bull and the rider and become the bull's new target.

5 For most people, taunting a hostile bull is the last thing in the world they'd want to do. But rodeo clowns seem to thrive on it. For them, getting trampled is a kind of rite of passage, separating the men from the boys. Wick Peth, an old rodeo clown, once said, "The best thing that can happen to a [rookie clown] is if he gets run over good the first few times out. It weeds them out fast. If a guy still thinks he wants to do it after that, he'll make it."

6 Rodeo clowns get banged up all the time. Injuries such as fractured fingers and toes are too minor to count. Ronny Sparks remembers only the serious ones. Over the years he has suffered a broken back, a broken collarbone, and a broken shoulder. Those injuries appear on just the first page of his medical history. Ronny also broke his tailbone twice, as well as his wrist, his ankle, and several ribs. And somewhere along the way, a bull knocked his teeth out. As one rodeo clown put it, "If you fight bulls, you're gonna get hurt just about every week."

7 Saving the fallen rider is only half the clown's job. Entertaining rodeo fans is the other half. Teasing the bull and dodging the charge isn't enough. Rodeo clowns have to make a show of it. Ronny Sparks and his twin brother, Donny, do that by jumping over the bull. Any mistake with this daring trick could be extremely painful, not to mention embarrassing. One time the bull lifted its head at just the wrong time, hooking Ronny's baggy pants and ripping them clean off.

8 Most rodeo clowns are young. It's not a job for older, slower men. By the time rodeo clowns are in their mid-thirties, they've either moved "into the barrel" or quit altogether.

9 There is always one rodeo clown who wears a barrel. He is—theoretically—safer than the clowns out in the open. The clown in the barrel looks most like a circus clown. He wears face makeup, a red nose, a colorful wig, maybe a goofy hat, and oversized clothes. He and his barrel become a kind of beach ball for angry bulls to toss.

10 The metal barrel is open at both ends. The inside is padded with foam and

A rodeo clown waits for some action at the Santa Barbara Old Spanish Days Fiesta.

equipped with hand grips. The grips allow the clown to pick up the 75-pound barrel and waddle around the ring. There is also a small ledge for the clown's feet. When the bull charges the barrel, the clown ducks his head inside and lifts his feet onto the ledge. A solid blow can send the barrel flying through the air. Inside the barrel, the clown holds on for dear life.

11 Being in the barrel carries its own risks. If the clown doesn't keep his teeth clenched, he could bite off his tongue when the bull tosses the barrel. Also, the barrel is open at both ends. The bull could easily ram one of its horns into either end. The clown must remember to tuck his head between his knees and lift his feet onto the ledge. Rudy Burns once forgot to tuck his head and it cost him a row of teeth. If you forget to lift your feet, says barrel clown Harold Murray, "the bull can snap both your ankles."

12 Crooked Nose, the most famous fighting bull of all time, was definitely not fond of barrels. At the age of two, he broke one of his horns on one. After that, Crooked Nose hated all barrels. He didn't just toss the barrel, he viciously attacked it. He often injured the clown inside. Once, he hooked a barrel with his horn and refused to let it go. It took the help of several people to save the clown trapped inside.

13 There is nothing quite like being a rodeo clown. Is there any other job in the world where you have to risk your life every day and make people laugh at the same time? Yet rodeo clowns live for the thrill of near misses. Besides, as barrel clown Martin Kiff once said, "[You get] the best seat in the house."

If you have been timed while reading this article, enter your reading time below. Then turn to the Words-per-Minute Table on page 71 and look up your reading speed (words per minute). Enter your reading speed on the graph on page 72.

Reading Time: Lesson 4

_______ : _______

Minutes *Seconds*

A Finding the Main Idea

One statement below expresses the main idea of the article. One statement is too general, or too broad. The other statement explains only part of the article; it is too narrow. Label the statements using the following key:

M—Main Idea **B—Too Broad** **N—Too Narrow**

_______ 1. The job of the rodeo clown is to distract the bull until the rodeo rider can run to safety.

_______ 2. Rodeo clowns risk their own safety while entertaining the fans and providing a way for riders to escape angry bulls.

_______ 3. Although the job of a rodeo clown looks like fun, it can also be dangerous.

_______ Score 15 points for a correct M answer.

_______ Score 5 points for each correct B or N answer.

_______ **Total Score:** Finding the Main Idea

B Recalling Facts

How well do you remember the facts in the article? Put an X in the box next to the answer that correctly completes each statement about the article.

1. After rodeo riders get off the bucking bull, the rodeo clowns
- ☐ a. taunt the bull and get it to charge toward them.
- ☐ b. place a barrel on the rider to protect him.
- ☐ c. fight the bull like a Spanish matador.

2. Rodeo clown Ronny Sparks's special trick is to
- ☐ a. jump over the bull.
- ☐ b. tease the bull.
- ☐ c. walk around in a barrel.

3. Most rodeo clowns quit the business around the age of
- ☐ a. 25.
- ☐ b. 35.
- ☐ c. 20.

4. When the bull charges the barrel, the clown should remember to
- ☐ a. shout loudly at the bull.
- ☐ b. wave a rag at the bull.
- ☐ c. duck his head and lift his feet.

5. A bull named Crooked Nose hated barrels after he
- ☐ a. hit his nose against one at the age of two.
- ☐ b. broke one of his horns on a barrel.
- ☐ c. broke his leg while kicking a barrel.

Score 5 points for each correct answer.

_______ **Total Score:** Recalling Facts

C Making Inferences

When you combine your own experience and information from a text to draw a conclusion that is not directly stated in that text, you are making an inference. Below are five statements that may or may not be inferences based on information in the article. Label the statements using the following key:

C—Correct Inference **F—Faulty Inference**

_______ 1. Rodeo riders become rodeo clowns when they get too old to ride.

_______ 2. Rodeo clowns need to be fast and creative.

_______ 3. Rodeo clowns need emergency medical treatment more often than the average person does.

_______ 4. Bulls enjoy being taunted and teased by rodeo clowns.

_______ 5. It is the dream of every rodeo clown to move "into the barrel" someday.

Score 5 points for each correct answer.

_______ **Total Score:** Making Inferences

D Using Words Precisely

Each numbered sentence below contains an underlined word or phrase from the article. Following the sentence are three definitions. One definition is closest to the meaning of the underlined word. One definition is opposite or nearly opposite. Label those two definitions using the following key. Do not label the remaining definition.

C—Closest **O—Opposite or Nearly Opposite**

1. These agile animals will stomp a fallen rider and try to gore him with their horns.

_______ a. slow-moving

_______ b. intelligent

_______ c. quick

2. For most people, taunting a hostile bull is the last thing in the world they'd want to do.

_______ a. unfriendly

_______ b. huge

_______ c. affectionate

3. He is—theoretically—safer than the clowns out in the open.

_______ a. luckily

_______ b. actually

_______ c. supposedly

4. If the clown doesn't keep his teeth clenched, he could bite off his tongue when the bull tosses the barrel.

_______ a. tightly closed

_______ b. open and relaxed

_______ c. clean

5. He didn't just toss the barrel, he viciously attacked it.

_______ a. later

_______ b. savagely

_______ c. gently

_______ Score 3 points for each correct C answer.

_______ Score 2 points for each correct O answer.

_______ **Total Score:** Using Words Precisely

Enter the four total scores in the spaces below, and add them together to find your Reading Comprehension Score. Then record your score on the graph on page 73.

Score	Question Type	Lesson 4
_______	Finding the Main Idea	
_______	Recalling Facts	
_______	Making Inferences	
_______	Using Words Precisely	
_______	**Reading Comprehension Score**	

Author's Approach

Put an X in the box next to the correct answer.

1. The main purpose of the first paragraph is to

☐ a. inform the reader about what bullfighters wear.

☐ b. contrast rodeo clowns and bullfighters.

☐ c. persuade the reader not to attend bullfights.

2. Choose the statement below that is the weakest argument for becoming a rodeo clown.

☐ a. You want to help keep rodeo riders safe.

☐ b. You want to feel the thrill of outwitting a bull.

☐ c. You want to wear a barrel.

3. What does the author imply by saying "Injuries such as fractured fingers and toes are too minor to count"?

☐ a. Rodeo clowns are embarrassed to admit that they sometimes break their fingers and toes.

☐ b. Rodeo clowns are too busy to bother treating their fractured fingers and toes.

☐ c. Rodeo clowns fracture their fingers and toes often and can withstand a great deal of pain.

4. Choose the statement below that best describes the author's position in paragraph 5.

☐ a. Good rodeo clowns must not be afraid of getting hurt.

☐ b. Rodeo clowns like to see each other get hurt.

☐ c. Rodeo clowns think that getting injured is fun.

_______ Number of correct answers

Record your personal assessment of your work on the Critical Thinking Chart on page 74.

Summarizing and Paraphrasing

Follow the directions provided for question 1. Put an X in the box next to the correct answer for the other questions.

1. Reread paragraph 9 in the article. Below, write a summary of the paragraph in no more than 25 words.

____

____

____

____

Reread your summary and decide whether it covers the important ideas in the paragraph. Next, decide how to shorten the summary to 15 words or less without leaving out any essential information. Write this summary below.

____

____

____

2. Read the statement below about the article. Then read the paraphrase of that statement. Choose the reason that best tells why the paraphrase does not say the same thing as the statement.

Statement: When the bull charges, the clown in the barrel must duck his head inside and lift his legs, or else he may be badly injured.

Paraphrase: The charging bull can hurt the clown in the barrel unless the clown pulls his legs into the barrel.

☐ a. Paraphrase says too much.
☐ b. Paraphrase doesn't say enough.
☐ c. Paraphrase doesn't agree with the statement about the article.

3. Choose the best one-sentence paraphrase for the following sentence from the article:

"Yet rodeo clowns live for the thrill of near misses."

☐ a. Rodeo clowns love the excitement that comes with injuries.
☐ b. Narrowly escaping danger is what makes rodeo clowns' lives worth living.
☐ c. Rodeo clowns would die if they couldn't avoid the bull's charge.

_______ Number of correct answers

Record your personal assessment of your work on the Critical Thinking Chart on page 74.

Critical Thinking

Follow the directions provided for questions 1, 2, and 5. Put an X in the box next to the correct answer for questions 3 and 4.

1. For each statement below, write O if it expresses an opinion or write F if it expresses a fact.

_______ a. Without rodeo clowns, going to a rodeo wouldn't be much fun.

_______ b. Rodeo riders try to stay on the bull for at least eight seconds.

_______ c. The rodeo clown who wears the barrel dresses up like a circus clown.

2. Choose from the letters below to correctly complete the following statement. Write the letters on the lines.

   In the article, _________ and _________ are different.

   a. the reason a horse kicks a rider
   b. the reason a bull kicks a rider
   c. the reason a bull attacks when someone invades his territory

3. What is a possible effect of the barrel clown's failure to keep his teeth tightly closed when the bull charges him?

   ☐ a. He could bite his tongue badly.
   ☐ b. He could get thrown out of the barrel.
   ☐ c. He could break his ankles.

4. How are rodeo clowns examples of daredevils?

   ☐ a. They are entertaining performers.
   ☐ b. They thrive on the danger of fighting angry bulls.
   ☐ c. They are tough and athletic.

5. In which paragraph did you find your information or details to answer question 2?

____

_________ Number of correct answers

Record your personal assessment of your work on the Critical Thinking Chart on page 74.

Personal Response

How do you think you would feel if you were facing an angry bull with only a barrel to protect yourself?

____

____

____

____

Self-Assessment

I'm proud of how I answered question # _________ in section _________ because

____

____

____

____

CHRISTIANE AMANPOUR
On the Front Lines

Christiane Amanpour stands next to the bullet-shattered window of her CNN van in Bosnia, February 1993.

Christiane Amanpour was asleep in her room at the Holiday Inn in Bosnia. Suddenly, an "awful whistling" noise startled her. A rocket shell smashed into the hotel two floors below her room. Luckily, the shell didn't explode. "Otherwise," she later said, "it would have been over for me."

2 Most people couldn't pack their bags fast enough to get out of the hotel. But Amanpour wasn't like most people. She had a job to do. She was covering the war in Bosnia as a foreign correspondent for CNN news, and she wasn't about to let a stray rocket scare her away. Her job was dangerous and she knew it. Once, her camera operator was hit by a bullet in the jaw. Amanpour knew she could be next. "But it never made me have second thoughts about doing my job here," she said. "I love my work."

3 Christiane Amanpour was born in London, England, in 1958. Her mother was English; her father was Iranian. Shortly after her birth, the family moved to Iran, where her father worked for an airline. The family had money and property. In her own words, Amanpour "lived a very privileged, Western-style life."

4 Even as a child, Amanpour showed signs of being a bit reckless. When she was five she climbed on a table to catch a

balloon that had floated to the ceiling. She ended up pulling down an entire chandelier. "I was scared of nothing," she recalled. "I rode full-size stallions and raced as a jockey. In fact, I won a first place cup once."

5 When she was 11, her parents sent Amanpour to a private school in England. Schoolwork was not her strong suit, however. She was homesick and hated the strict discipline. At one time she had hoped to become a doctor, but her poor grades made that impossible. So after high school, Amanpour took a job in a department store. Her life seemed to be going nowhere. Then she got a break. One of her sisters had been accepted into a school of journalism. When the sister suddenly decided not to go, Amanpour saw a new chance for herself. She asked if the school would take her instead. The school agreed.

6 In 1979, a radical new government took over in Iran. One year later, war broke out between Iran and Iraq. Amanpour's family was in London at the time. They decided to wait out the war in England. Soon, the Amanpours had lost all their property. They had to start over from scratch. But the experience gave Christiane a clear vision of her future. "From that moment," she said, "I knew I wanted to be a foreign correspondent. If I was going to be affected by events, I wanted to be a part of them."

7 Amanpour decided to pursue her studies in the United States. She enrolled at the University of Rhode Island. There she turned out to be a fine student. She worked hard and in 1983 graduated at the top of her class. While at school, she worked part-time for a small radio station. She also worked at a local TV station.

8 Christiane kept her TV job for a few months after college. But she longed to work on a larger stage. So the fall after graduation she applied for a job at CNN, a new national station. The all-news network gave her work, but it wasn't very glamorous. "It was the lowest job," she recalled, "but I came in on weekends on my own and practiced writing... scripts."

Christiane Amanpour arrived in the Persian Gulf as soon as word got out of the Iraqi invasion of Kuwait. Here, the streets of Kuwait City are deserted after the invasion.

[9] Although Amanpour let everyone at CNN know about her ambition, the people there just shrugged their shoulders. No one encouraged her. "She said she wanted to be a star," said Eason Jordan, one of her bosses. "We all smiled." They knew that becoming a foreign correspondent wasn't easy for anyone. There were lots of candidates and few openings. But Amanpour never lost sight of her goal. In 1985, she got the chance she needed. CNN planned to do a special show on Iran. She asked to take part. Since she spoke Farsi, the language of Iran, CNN allowed her to help. Her work impressed her bosses and she won a promotion to the New York office.

[10] In 1990, a CNN job opened in Germany. It was offered to several more experienced reporters. They all turned it down. When Amanpour lobbied for the job, CNN gave it to her. At last, she had reached her goal. She was a foreign correspondent.

[11] Amanpour made a solid impression right away. She had been in Germany just a few days when she flew to Romania. She went there to cover that nation's first free election. But she found a bigger story. She discovered that the orphanages were a filthy disgrace. Many children had been left naked with little food or medicine. Her reports produced worldwide sympathy for these children.

[12] Next, Amanpour went to the Persian Gulf. Iraq had just invaded Kuwait, its tiny neighbor. She was one of the first reporters on the scene. She saw the Iraqi tanks crush Kuwait. She stayed in the region to report on the Persian Gulf War that followed. In that war, the United States and its allies drove Iraq out of Kuwait. Amanpour did not play it safe. She went to Baghdad, the capital of Iraq, to report on American bombing raids.

[13] Such courage won Amanpour fans around the world. Over 140 million people from more than 200 countries watched her. She always seemed to be in the thick of the world's hottest trouble spots. "Christiane's fearless," said Ed Turner, her CNN boss. "Somalia, Russia, the gulf, Bosnia—she's done it all. But she worries me because she thinks bullets bounce off her."

[14] That was not quite true. Amanpour was a daredevil, but she wasn't crazy. When she was on the front lines, she always wore a helmet and a flak vest, just as the other reporters did. Still, such safeguards didn't always offer enough protection. At least 35 journalists were killed in less than two years during the civil war in Bosnia.

[15] It sometimes seemed that Amanpour had a sixth sense for danger. As Allison Biello, a colleague who worked with her in Romania, put it, "Christiane's like a cat. She's got the best instincts for knowing when to get in and out."

[16] One of her idols was Peter Jennings, the long-time ABC-TV anchorman. By 1993, she had become one of his heroes. "She's brave, she's intelligent—she should work for us!" he said.

[17] Despite huge salary offers from other networks, Amanpour has stayed with CNN. She continues to report from the world's worst trouble spots. She knows the risks. But she doesn't let that stop her. "I have no romantic ideas of being killed or wounded in the line of duty," she has said, "but I'm not afraid of it either."

If you have been timed while reading this article, enter your reading time below. Then turn to the Words-per-Minute Table on page 71 and look up your reading speed (words per minute). Enter your reading speed on the graph on page 72.

Reading Time: Lesson 5

________ : ________

Minutes *Seconds*

A Finding the Main Idea

One statement below expresses the main idea of the article. One statement is too general, or too broad. The other statement explains only part of the article; it is too narrow. Label the statements using the following key:

M—Main Idea **B—Too Broad** **N—Too Narrow**

_______ 1. Reporters who work in trouble spots around the world often face danger as part of their jobs.

_______ 2. Reporter Christiane Amanpour's instinct for news led her to Bosnia, where a fierce civil war was raging.

_______ 3. Reporter Christiane Amanpour can always be counted on to report on world news, not allowing danger to stop her from gathering information.

_______ Score 15 points for a correct M answer.

_______ Score 5 points for each correct B or N answer.

_______ **Total Score:** Finding the Main Idea

B Recalling Facts

How well do you remember the facts in the article? Put an X in the box next to the answer that correctly completes each statement about the article.

1. Christiane Amanpour was born in
- ☐ a. Iran.
- ☐ b. England.
- ☐ c. Iraq.

2. After her family lost its money, Amanpour dreamed of becoming a
- ☐ a. banker.
- ☐ b. politician.
- ☐ c. foreign correspondent.

3. During the war in Bosnia, Amanpour worked for
- ☐ a. BBC.
- ☐ b. CNN.
- ☐ c. NBC.

4. Amanpour was one of the first reporters to see Iraqi tanks entering
- ☐ a. Kuwait.
- ☐ b. Iran.
- ☐ c. Bosnia.

5. To protect herself on the front lines, Amanpour
- ☐ a. wore a helmet and flak vest.
- ☐ b. carried a high-powered rifle.
- ☐ c. displayed her reporter's ID card and a white flag.

Score 5 points for each correct answer.

_______ **Total Score:** Recalling Facts

C Making Inferences

When you combine your own experience and information from a text to draw a conclusion that is not directly stated in that text, you are making an inference. Below are five statements that may or may not be inferences based on information in the article. Label the statements using the following key:

C—Correct Inference **F—Faulty Inference**

_______ 1. To become a doctor, you need to get good grades in school.

_______ 2. Women make better foreign correspondents than men do.

_______ 3. During the time when bombing raids were taking place in Baghdad, no one was allowed to enter or leave the city.

_______ 4. Orphanages in Romania are worse than those in any other country.

_______ 5. News reporters pay close attention to what their fellow reporters are doing.

Score 5 points for each correct answer.

_______ **Total Score:** Making Inferences

D Using Words Precisely

Each numbered sentence below contains an underlined word or phrase from the article. Following the sentence are three definitions. One definition is closest to the meaning of the underlined word. One definition is opposite or nearly opposite. Label those two definitions using the following key. Do not label the remaining definition.

C—Closest **O—Opposite or Nearly Opposite**

1. In her own words, Amanpour "lived a very privileged, Western-style life."

_______ a. disadvantaged

_______ b. sheltered

_______ c. favored

2. In 1979, a radical new government took over in Iran.

_______ a. revolutionary

_______ b. moderate

_______ c. dangerous

3. Her work impressed her bosses and she won a promotion to the New York office.

_______ a. lower, less important job

_______ b. trip

_______ c. higher position

4. When Amanpour lobbied for the job, CNN gave it to her.

_______ a. noticed

_______ b. strongly requested

_______ c. expressed distaste for

5. "I have no romantic ideas of being killed or wounded in the line of duty," she said, "but I'm not afraid of it either."

_______ a. foreign

_______ b. dreamy

_______ c. realistic

_______ Score 3 points for each correct C answer.

_______ Score 2 points for each correct O answer.

_______ **Total Score:** Using Words Precisely

Enter the four total scores in the spaces below, and add them together to find your Reading Comprehension Score. Then record your score on the graph on page 73.

Score	Question Type	Lesson 5
_______	Finding the Main Idea	
_______	Recalling Facts	
_______	Making Inferences	
_______	Using Words Precisely	
_______	**Reading Comprehension Score**	

Author's Approach

Put an X in the box next to the correct answer.

1. The main purpose of the first paragraph is to

☐ a. inform readers that there is a Holiday Inn in Bosnia.

☐ b. describe the sound of a rocket shell crashing.

☐ c. give an example of the dangers Amanpour faced.

2. Which of the following statements from the article best describes Amanpour's childhood?

☐ a. "Her life seemed to be going nowhere."

☐ b. "The family had money and property. In her own words, Amanpour 'lived a very privileged, Western-style life.'"

☐ c. "Amanpour decided to pursue her studies in the United States."

3. Judging by statements from the article "Christiane Amanpour: On the Front Lines," you can conclude that the author wants the reader to think that

☐ a. Amanpour is both brave and sensible when she goes after a story.

☐ b. Amanpour pays no attention to her own safety when she wants a news story.

☐ c. Amanpour was reckless as a child, and even more reckless as an adult.

4. In this article, "It sometimes seemed that Amanpour had a sixth sense for danger" means

☐ a. Amanpour always felt that she was in danger.

☐ b. Amanpour was good at sensing when danger was approaching.

☐ c. Amanpour looked for danger because she enjoyed it.

_______ Number of correct answers

Record your personal assessment of your work on the Critical Thinking Chart on page 74.

Summarizing and Paraphrasing

Put an X in the box next to the correct answer.

1. Below are summaries of the article. Choose the summary that says all the most important things about the article but in the fewest words.

☐ a. Reporter Christiane Amanpour is well known for her ability to cover world news in spite of any danger.

☐ b. CNN news reporter Christiane Amanpour first became well known internationally when she told the world about the disgraceful conditions in Bosnian orphanages. Since then, she has covered many other world events.

☐ c. Daughter of an English mother and an Iranian father, Christiane Amanpour is willing to put herself in danger to cover breaking stories anywhere around the world, including war-torn areas such as Romania, Bosnia, and Iraq.

2. Read the statement about the article below. Then read the paraphrase of that statement. Choose the reason that best tells why the paraphrase does not say the same thing as the statement.

Statement: People shrugged and smiled when Amanpour said she wanted to be a star because they knew that becoming a foreign correspondent isn't easy.

Paraphrase: People believed that Amanpour had no chance to become a famous foreign correspondent.

☐ a. Paraphrase says too much.

☐ b. Paraphrase doesn't say enough.

☐ c. Paraphrase doesn't agree with the statement about the article.

3. Choose the sentence that correctly restates the following sentence from the article:

"Most people couldn't pack their bags fast enough to get out of the hotel."

☐ a. The reaction of most people would have been to get out the hotel as quickly as possible.

☐ b. Most of the guests in the hotel were not able to pack their suitcases fast enough to avoid injury.

☐ c. Most hotel guests packed their bags and checked out of the hotel quickly.

________ Number of correct answers

Record your personal assessment of your work on the Critical Thinking Chart on page 74.

Critical Thinking

Put an X in the box next to the correct answer for questions 1, 2, and 4. Follow the directions provided for questions 3 and 5.

1. Which of the following statements from the article is an opinion rather than a fact?

☐ a. "She's brave, she's intelligent—she should work for us!"

☐ b. "She went to Baghdad, the capital of Iraq, to report on American bombing raids."

☐ c. "She worked hard and in 1983 graduated at the top of her class."

2. From the article, you can predict that if Amanpour ever loses her job with CNN, she will

☐ a. move back to Iran to get back her family's money.
☐ b. be offered a job with another network.
☐ c. stop putting herself in danger.

3. Think about cause-effect relationships in the article. Fill in the blanks in the cause-effect chart, drawing from the letters below.

Cause	Effect
Amanpour received poor grades.	________
Amanpour's family was hurt by events in Iran.	________
________	CNN officials let her work on a show about Iran.

a. Amanpour couldn't become a doctor.
b. Amanpour knew Farsi.
c. Amanpour decided to become a foreign correspondent.

4. If you were a news reporter, how could you use the information in the article to report on a dangerous event?

☐ a. Like Amanpour, respect the danger but don't let it stop you from doing your job.
☐ b. Like Amanpour, get a job with CNN.
☐ c. Like Amanpour, learn to speak Farsi.

5. Which paragraphs from the article provide evidence that supports your answer to question 3?

____

________ Number of correct answers

Record your personal assessment of your work on the Critical Thinking Chart on page 74.

Personal Response

If I were the author, I would add

____

____

____

____

because

____

____

____

____

Self-Assessment

I was confused on question # ________ in section ________ because

____

____

____

____

EDMUND HILLARY & TENZING NORGAY

Conquering Everest

Edmund Hillary slowly led the way down the mountain from Camp Two to Camp One. Tenzing Norgay, who was roped to Hillary, followed behind. The two men were weaving their way between huge towers of ice. Suddenly, the snow under Hillary's feet gave way. He fell into a what seemed like a bottomless crevasse. "Tenzing! Tenzing!" he shouted.

2 As Hillary fell, Tenzing jammed his ice axe into the snow and threw himself down beside it. Luckily, the rope and the axe held. Hillary wound up dangling 15 feet down inside the crevasse. It took all of Tenzing's strength to haul Hillary up. The strain on his hands was so great that it ripped holes in his gloves. But, thankfully, Tenzing managed to pull his climbing partner out of the crevasse to safety. Back at Camp One, Hillary told everyone, "Without Tenzing I would have been finished today."

3 Hillary and Tenzing were part of a British mountain climbing expedition. Their goal was to reach the summit of Mount Everest, the highest peak in the world. No one had ever climbed the

Mt. Everest, situated on the border of Tibet and Nepal, is the world's highest mountain at 29,028 feet.

29,028-foot monster. Over the past 30 years, at least 10 other expeditions had tried. Some had come close, but in the end they had all failed to reach the top. Along the way, several climbers and their guides had died. But now, in May 1953, Hillary and Tenzing hoped to be the ones who made it. Tenzing, who had tried and failed to climb to the summit six times before, later said, "Only one thing... mattered to me. And that was Everest. To *climb* Everest."

4 Hillary, an Englishman, was a beekeeper by profession. He climbed mountains for fun. Tenzing, on the other hand, climbed mountains for a living. Tenzing was a Sherpa, one of the rugged mountain people who live in Nepal. Sherpas became famous as porters and guides to those who wanted to climb in the Himalayan Mountains. Tenzing, it was said, was "the toughest of a tough race." His adventures in the mountains earned him the nickname "Tiger of the Snows."

5 Tenzing once wrote, "The man has never been born, of course, who does not have some difficulties on a peak like Everest." One of the difficulties is simply breathing. Above 20,000 feet, the air is very thin. Most climbers bring their own supply of oxygen. Even so, they suffer headaches, sore throats, and nausea. They lose their appetite. Sleeplessness is such a problem that many climbers take sleeping pills.

6 Exhaustion and frostbite can defeat any climber. And the threat of accidental death is always present. Death might come from an avalanche, a falling boulder, or "bad snow." "Bad snow" is snow over a deep crevasse that won't support the weight of a human being. Storms are another danger. A climber who gets caught in a storm and can't get back to camp before nightfall is in big trouble.

7 Hillary and Tenzing knew that climbing Everest would be a monumental task. They couldn't possibly do it alone. It took a total team effort. Their team was made up of a dozen climbers as well as 20 Sherpas. The overall leader of the attempt was Colonel John Hunt. He was the one who made the final decisions. And he was the one who decided that Tenzing and Hillary should be the two to try for the summit.

8 The climbers had to set up a series of camps along the route to the summit. First, they set up Camp One. The team used this as a base for setting up Camp Two. That then became the base for establishing Camp Three and so forth. There was a lot of traveling back and forth between the camps. Naturally, the wind, cold, and snow made the higher camps more difficult to establish.

9 Slowly, the members of the team thinned out. Most of them dropped out by design, but some members unexpectedly got sick and had to quit early. By the time the team established Camp Seven, there were only 19 members left. By Camp Eight, at 27,500 feet, the number had dropped to six. And the plan for Camp

Sir Edmund Hillary and Tenzing Norgay at their camp 27,000 feet up Everest the day before reaching the peak in 1953

Nine, the last camp, called for just two members. These two would be Tenzing and Hillary.

10 On May 28, Tenzing, Hillary, and three others headed up the ice and snow to set up Camp Nine. The other climbers carried the vital supplies Tenzing and Hillary would need. Then they returned to Camp Eight to wait. Meanwhile, Tenzing and Hillary hacked a space barely large enough to pitch a tent. Then they tried—without much luck—to sleep. They would make their assault on the summit the following day.

11 The two men got up at 3:30 the next morning. The weather was calm and clear. At this altitude, however, the brain works slowly. Everything takes at least five times as long to do. It took three hours for the men to thaw out boots, get dressed, and check their equipment. So Tenzing and Hillary didn't crawl out of their tent until 6:30.

12 The final climb was an arduous step-by-step test of endurance and courage. First Hillary led the way, cutting steps in the snow. Then Tenzing took over the lead. The two kept switching back and forth to conserve their energy. At one point, they encountered "an almost vertical white wall." The snow was not firm; it kept crumbling as they tried to scale it. Tenzing later wrote, "It was one of the most dangerous places I had ever been on a mountain. Even now, when I think of it, I can still feel as I felt then, and the hair almost stands up on the back of my hands."

13 Somehow they made it up past the wall of snow. Now they had only a 300-foot ridge to cross. On the left side there was an 8,000-foot drop. The right side was covered with snow cornices hanging out over a 10,000-foot drop. Tenzing and Hillary wisely stuck to the middle of the ridge. At 11:30 A.M. that day—May 29, 1953—they stepped together onto the summit of Mount Everest.

14 On the summit, Tenzing Norgay buried some sweets. Sherpas sometimes offer sweets to those who are near and dear to them. Tenzing felt that Everest was like a special friend. As he covered his offering, he made a silent prayer. "Seven times I had come to the mountain of my dream," he later wrote, "and on this, the seventh, with God's help, the dream had come true."

If you have been timed while reading this article, enter your reading time below. Then turn to the Words-per-Minute Table on page 71 and look up your reading speed (words per minute). Enter your reading speed on the graph on page 72.

Reading Time: Lesson 6

________ : ________

Minutes *Seconds*

A Finding the Main Idea

One statement below expresses the main idea of the article. One statement is too general, or too broad. The other statement explains only part of the article; it is too narrow. Label the statements using the following key:

M—Main Idea **B—Too Broad** **N—Too Narrow**

______ 1. Determination and hard work helped Tenzing Norgay and Edmund Hillary conquer Mount Everest, the world's highest peak.

______ 2. Climbers on very high mountains often suffer headaches, sore throats, nausea, and sleeplessness, as Edmund Hillary and Tenzing Norgay discovered.

______ 3. Mountain climbing is a dangerous occupation, especially on very high peaks.

______ Score 15 points for a correct M answer.

______ Score 5 points for each correct B or N answer.

______ **Total Score:** Finding the Main Idea

B Recalling Facts

How well do you remember the facts in the article? Put an X in the box next to the answer that correctly completes each statement about the article.

1. Hillary and Norgay were part of an expedition from
   - ☐ a. the United States.
   - ☐ b. Switzerland.
   - ☐ c. Great Britain.

2. Mount Everest is located in the
   - ☐ a. Rocky Mountains.
   - ☐ b. Alps.
   - ☐ c. Himalayas.

3. The rugged mountain people of Nepal are known as
   - ☐ a. Tigers of the Snows.
   - ☐ b. Sherpas.
   - ☐ c. Inuits.

4. The last camp, Camp Nine, gave shelter to
   - ☐ a. two climbers.
   - ☐ b. six climbers.
   - ☐ c. 19 climbers.

5. The climbers reached Everest's summit in
   - ☐ a. 1953.
   - ☐ b. 1989.
   - ☐ c. 1913.

Score 5 points for each correct answer.

______ **Total Score:** Recalling Facts

C Making Inferences

When you combine your own experience and information from a text to draw a conclusion that is not directly stated in that text, you are making an inference. Below are five statements that may or may not be inferences based on information in the article. Label the statements using the following key:

C—Correct Inference **F—Faulty Inference**

_______ 1. All residents of Nepal are excellent mountain climbers.

_______ 2. Humans need an ample supply of oxygen to feel their best.

_______ 3. Colonel John Hunt thought that Hillary and Norgay, of all the men in the expedition, had the best chance of reaching the summit.

_______ 4. When you climb very high peaks, you should give yourself plenty of time to do even the simplest tasks.

_______ 5. Mount Everest has never been successfully climbed since Hillary and Norgay conquered it in 1953.

Score 5 points for each correct answer.

_______ **Total Score:** Making Inferences

D Using Words Precisely

Each numbered sentence below contains an underlined word or phrase from the article. Following the sentence are three definitions. One definition is closest to the meaning of the underlined word. One definition is opposite or nearly opposite. Label those two definitions using the following key. Do not label the remaining definition.

C—Closest **O—Opposite or Nearly Opposite**

1. Hillary and Norgay knew that climbing Everest would be a <u>monumental</u> task.

_______ a. huge and overwhelming

_______ b. discouraging

_______ c. small and easy to handle

2. Most of them dropped out <u>by design</u>, but some members unexpectedly got sick and had to quit early.

_______ a. beautifully

_______ b. by surprise

_______ c. as planned before

3. The other climbers carried the <u>vital</u> supplies Norgay and Hillary would need.

_______ a. cooking

_______ b. essential

_______ c. unnecessary

4. The final climb was an <u>arduous</u> step-by-step test of endurance.

_______ a. impossible

_______ b. easy

_______ c. strenuous, difficult

5. The two kept switching back and forth to conserve their energy.

_______ a. save

_______ b. use up

_______ c. enjoy

_______ Score 3 points for each correct C answer.

_______ Score 2 points for each correct O answer.

_______ **Total Score:** Using Words Precisely

Enter the four total scores in the spaces below, and add them together to find your Reading Comprehension Score. Then record your score on the graph on page 73.

Score	Question Type	Lesson 6
_______	Finding the Main Idea	
_______	Recalling Facts	
_______	Making Inferences	
_______	Using Words Precisely	
_______	**Reading Comprehension Score**	

Author's Approach

Put an X in the box next to the correct answer.

1. What is the author's purpose in writing "Edmund Hillary and Tenzing Norgay: Conquering Everest"?

☐ a. To encourage the reader to take up mountain climbing

☐ b. To inform the reader about two climbers who accomplished a tremendous feat of skill and courage

☐ c. To emphasize the differences between British and Sherpa mountain climbers

2. From the statements below, choose those that you believe the author would agree with.

☐ a. Mountain climbing is serious business that should be approached with attention to detail.

☐ b. Those who climb mountains are foolishly risking their lives for no good reason.

☐ c. Successful mountain climbing requires cooperation from all members of the climbing team.

3. Judging by statements from the article "Edmund Hillary and Tenzing Norgay: Conquering Everest," you can conclude that the author wants the reader to think that

☐ a. Norgay was a better climber than Hillary.

☐ b. Norgay and Hillary were about equal in their climbing ability.

☐ c. Hillary was a better climber than Norgay.

_______ Number of correct answers

Record your personal assessment of your work on the Critical Thinking Chart on page 74.

Summarizing and Paraphrasing

Follow the directions provided for questions 1 and 2.

1. Complete the following one-sentence summary of the article using the lettered phrases from the phrase bank below. Write the letters on the lines.

Phrase Bank:
a. a description of a dangerous climbing accident
b. how the team faced the many challenges of climbing Everest
c. Hillary and Norgay reaching the summit

The article about Edmund Hillary and Tenzing Norgay's ascent of Mount Everest begins with________, goes on to explain________, and ends with________.

2. Reread paragraph 7 in the article. Below, write a summary of the paragraph in no more than 25 words.

____

____

____

____

Reread your summary and decide whether it covers the important ideas in the paragraph. Next, decide how to shorten the summary to 15 words or less without leaving out any essential information. Write this summary below.

____

____

________ Number of correct answers

Record your personal assessment of your work on the Critical Thinking Chart on page 74.

Critical Thinking

Put an X in the box next to the correct answer for questions 1, 4, and 5. Follow the directions provided for questions 2 and 3.

1. Judging by the events in the article, you can predict that the following will happen next:

☐ a. Hillary and Norgay will set up camp and spend several days at the summit of Mount Everest.

☐ b. Hillary and Norgay will die on the way down the mountain.

☐ c. As soon as possible, Hillary and Norgay will leave the summit and rejoin the members of the climbing party at a lower camp before descending the mountain.

2. Using what you know about Edmund Hillary and what is told about Tenzing Norgay in the article, name three ways Edmund Hillary is similar to and three ways Edmund Hillary is different from Tenzing Norgay. Cite the paragraph number(s) where you found details in the article to support your conclusions.

Similarities

____

____

____

Differences

____

____

____

3. Read paragraph 5. Then choose from the letters below to correctly complete the following statement. Write the letters on the lines.

   According to paragraph 5, ________ because ________.

   a. mountain air doesn't have enough oxygen
   b. climbers feel sick on mountains
   c. Norgay later wrote about his experiences on Everest

4. Of the following theme categories, which would this story fit into?
- ☐ a. Nature is always kind.
- ☐ b. If you keep trying, you will succeed.
- ☐ c. Depend only upon yourself if you want to succeed.

5. What did you have to do to answer question 3?
- ☐ a. find an opinion (what someone thinks about something)
- ☐ b. find a description (how something looks)
- ☐ c. find an effect (something that happened)

________ Number of correct answers

Record your personal assessment of your work on the Critical Thinking Chart on page 74.

Personal Response

I wonder why

____

____

____

____

Self-Assessment

When reading the article, I was having trouble with

____

____

____

____

CRAIG BREEDLOVE

Speed on Wheels

Craig Breedlove's thrust car, Spirit of America, breaks the sound barrier, September 1997.

As Craig Breedlove once said, "You have to be careful which way you point it because it will go there." He was talking about his car, *Spirit of America*. Well, it wasn't really a car. Certainly it was nothing like the family Ford or Chevy. No, Breedlove's car was more like a jet plane on wheels. It was built for speed, and Breedlove used it to see just how fast he could go.

2 Ever since Craig Breedlove was a young boy he had been obsessed with speed. In 1950, at the age of 13, he built his first hot rod. Four years later, Breedlove took up car racing. He once crashed a friend's souped-up 1932 Chevy at 120 miles per hour (m.p.h.). The crash threw Breedlove through the car's cloth roof. Somehow, he lived to tell the tale.

3 Soon after that incident, Breedlove took up the challenge of pure speed. In 1961 he bought a surplus jet engine for $500. It became the engine for his first *Spirit of America* car. Two years later, he drove the car to a new land speed mark of 407 m.p.h. The record didn't last long. That same year, Art Arfons, driving his *Green Monster*, went 434 m.p.h. Over the next several years, the two speedsters battled back and forth. First one would

break the record and then the other.

4 More than once, Breedlove flirted with disaster. In 1964, he flashed across the salt flats in Utah at 526 m.p.h. But going that fast was only half the challenge. Stopping was the other half. Cars that go this fast need parachutes to slow them down. But this time, as he tried to slow down, Breedlove lost both his parachutes. He also burned out his brakes. The car roared past the braking area and smashed through a telephone pole. (The power company later sent him a bill for $200.) The car then flew through the air and landed nose-first in an 18-foot-deep pond. In danger of drowning, Breedlove managed to scramble out of the car. He then swam to shore unhurt.

5 A few days later, Arfons set a new world record. Breedlove came back the next year with an all-new *Spirit of America*. He set a higher record with a speed of 555 m.p.h. The stubborn Arfons then took the lead again with an awesome 576 m.p.h. But Breedlove did him one better. He became the first man in history to go 600 m.p.h. on land.

6 Art Arfons could never beat that mark. But others did. Gary Gabelich went 622 m.p.h. in his *Blue Flame* rocket car. Then, in 1983, his record was broken by an Englishman named Richard Noble. Noble's new world mark was 633 m.p.h.

7 By this time, Craig Breedlove had gone on to other activities. He had lost his sponsor, Goodyear Tires, and had given up his quest to hold the land speed record. For a few years, he switched to quarter-mile drag racing. In this field, too, he set new speed records. And again he cheated death. He once flipped his dragster at 420 m.p.h. and walked away. At last, in 1976, he quit. It seemed that his racing days were over.

8 But Breedlove's desire for pure speed never left him. In 1993, he was back on the track. He was now in his late 50s. He had more cash, having made money selling real estate. Also, Breedlove had a new sponsor, Shell Oil. He returned to racing with three goals in mind. First, he thought, he would break Noble's speed record, which still stood at 633 m.p.h. Next he would become the first racer to top the 700 m.p.h. mark. And finally he would break the 760-mile-per-hour sound barrier.

9 As before, there were not many rules for Breedlove to worry about. In this sport, there aren't any limits to the size, shape, or power of the car. To set a new mark, however, a couple of standards must be met. The car must race through a measured mile "speed trap" where the speed is measured. The car must then be turned around and raced back through the "speed trap" in the other direction. This eliminates tailwind as a factor in the car's speed. Both runs must be made within one hour. The official speed is based on the average of the two runs.

10 Rocket-powered cars such as Breedlove's need about six miles to reach

Craig Breedlove and his car, Spirit of America

top speed. They then need another six miles to slow down. To be on the safe side, two more miles are added to each end of the course. There are only a few places on earth that are suited for such speeds. The best place is the flat and barren Black Rock desert in Nevada.

11 By 1996, Breedlove had a new *Spirit of America* car. The gleaming white vehicle was 44 feet long with an engine that came from a U.S. Navy Phantom jet fighter. Normally, such an engine produces 17,000 pounds of thrust. Breedlove made it even more powerful. When he was finished, it could generate 22,650 pounds of thrust. That's about the same as 45,000 horsepower! (In comparison, a typical car has about 140 horsepower.)

12 The shape of the car had to be carefully planned. That's because when it approaches the sound barrier, a car creates shock waves. Such waves, said one design expert, are "so powerful they can flatten wood-frame buildings." The design had to deflect these shock waves up and away from the car.

13 On October 28, 1996, the 59-year-old Breedlove was ready. He squeezed into the cockpit. Despite the car's length, there wasn't much room for the driver. The *Spirit of America* was mostly fuel and engine. At first, everything went well. When the car hit the "speed trap," it zoomed up to 675 m.p.h.

14 Then, in an instant, something went wrong. Strong crosswinds hit the car and shock waves began to buffet the cockpit. Breedlove knew he had to stop, so he quickly hit the "kill switch." But he was going far too fast. The car flipped onto its side and careened across the desert, making a broad U-turn. The *Spirit of America* barely missed a crowd of spectators who had come to watch. It almost smashed into a parked van. When it finally came to rest, the car was 2.7 miles off course. Luckily, however, no one was killed.

15 Amazingly, Breedlove escaped serious injury. "It just got away from me, but I'm all right," he said. Still, it was a bitter disappointment. He had gone faster than Noble. But since the car was wrecked, he couldn't make the second run. Craig Breedlove would have to wait for another day.

16 That day may never come. On September 26, 1997, Andy Green raised the bar again. Driving Richard Noble's car, he set a new land speed record. His average for two runs was 714 m.p.h. That broke Noble's old record by more than 80 m.p.h. A few weeks later, Green broke the sound barrier by driving through the "speed trap" at 762 m.p.h.. His feat did not become an official record because he was a minute late making the return trip. Still, Green had done what Breedlove had always hoped to do.

17 It was hard for Breedlove to see Green succeed where he had failed. But Breedlove could look back on a career of many accomplishments. After all, he had been the first to go 400 m.p.h. He had also been the first to go 500 m.p.h. and 600 m.p.h. So while he would not be the first to go faster than 700 m.p.h., he would long be remembered as a giant in land speed racing.

If you have been timed while reading this article, enter your reading time below. Then turn to the Words-per-Minute Table on page 71 and look up your reading speed (words per minute). Enter your reading speed on the graph on page 72.

Reading Time: Lesson 7

_______ : _______

Minutes *Seconds*

A Finding the Main Idea

One statement below expresses the main idea of the article. One statement is too general, or too broad. The other statement explains only part of the article; it is too narrow. Label the statements using the following key:

M—Main Idea **B—Too Broad** **N—Too Narrow**

_______ 1. A number of skilled and daring drivers dream of setting land speed records with their souped-up cars.

_______ 2. In 1961, Craig Breedlove set the land speed record with a car that was outfitted with a jet engine.

_______ 3. For years, Craig Breedlove set one land speed record after another with his superfast, jet-engine-powered cars.

_______ Score 15 points for a correct M answer.

_______ Score 5 points for each correct B or N answer.

_______ **Total Score:** Finding the Main Idea

B Recalling Facts

How well do you remember the facts in the article? Put an X in the box next to the answer that correctly completes each statement about the article.

1. The name of Craig Breedlove's car was

☐ a. *The Spirit of St. Louis.*
☐ b. *Spirit of America.*
☐ c. *Blue Flame.*

2. In the early years, Breedlove's major rival was

☐ a. Art Arfons.
☐ b. Richard Green.
☐ c. Andy Green.

3. To set a record, a car must race through a measured mile called a

☐ a. sound barrier.
☐ b. race course.
☐ c. speed trap.

4. In its last outing in 1996, *Spirit of America* reached a speed of

☐ a. 407 miles per hour
☐ b. 500 miles per hour.
☐ c. 675 miles per hour.

5. At the time of his last try at breaking the land speed record, Breedlove was

☐ a. 48 years old.
☐ b. 59 years old.
☐ c. 75 years old.

Score 5 points for each correct answer.

_______ **Total Score:** Recalling Facts

C Making Inferences

When you combine your own experience and information from a text to draw a conclusion that is not directly stated in that text, you are making an inference. Below are five statements that may or may not be inferences based on information in the article. Label the statements using the following key:

C—Correct Inference **F—Faulty Inference**

_______ 1. Breedlove was the first person ever to put a jet engine into a car.

_______ 2. Craig Breedlove and Art Arfons were good friends.

_______ 3. It takes a great deal of money to outfit vehicles to break land speed records.

_______ 4. When observing attempts at breaking the land speed record, it is a good idea to stand at least a few miles away from the action.

_______ 5. Cars such as *Spirit of America* must pass strict inspections to make sure they meet official league standards.

Score 5 points for each correct answer.

_______ **Total Score:** Making Inferences

D Using Words Precisely

Each numbered sentence below contains an underlined word or phrase from the article. Following the sentence are three definitions. One definition is closest to the meaning of the underlined word. One definition is opposite or nearly opposite. Label those two definitions using the following key. Do not label the remaining definition.

C—Closest **O—Opposite or Nearly Opposite**

1. Ever since Craig Breedlove was a young boy he had been obsessed with speed.

_______ a. taken over by

_______ b. bored with

_______ c. frightened by

2. In 1961 he bought a surplus jet engine for $500.

_______ a. needed

_______ b. powerful

_______ c. leftover

3. This eliminates tailwind as a factor in the car's speed.

_______ a. inserts

_______ b. discusses

_______ c. removes

4. The design had to deflect these shock waves up and away from the car.

_______ a. attract

_______ b. turn aside

_______ c. expect

5. Strong crosswinds hit the car and shock waves began to buffet the cockpit.

_______ a. hit just once

_______ b. hit repeatedly

_______ c. destroy

_______ Score 3 points for each correct C answer.

_______ Score 2 points for each correct O answer.

_______ **Total Score:** Using Words Precisely

Enter the four total scores in the spaces below, and add them together to find your Reading Comprehension Score. Then record your score on the graph on page 73.

Score	Question Type	Lesson 7
_______	Finding the Main Idea	
_______	Recalling Facts	
_______	Making Inferences	
_______	Using Words Precisely	
_______	**Reading Comprehension Score**	

Author's Approach

Put an X in the box next to the correct answer.

1. The author uses the first sentence of the article to

☐ a. create a mood of fear.

☐ b. raise the reader's curiosity about what Craig Breedlove is referring to when he talks about "it."

☐ c. compare *Spirit of America* and normal cars.

2. How is the author's purpose for writing the article expressed in paragraph 17?

☐ a. The paragraph reminds the reader that Breedlove had been the first to go 400 m.p.h.

☐ b. The paragraph tells the reader that Breedlove was disappointed that someone succeeded where he had failed.

☐ c. The paragraph states that Breedlove will be "remembered as a giant in land speed racing."

3. Choose the statement below that best describes the author's position in paragraph 4.

☐ a. Breedlove was sometimes amazingly lucky.

☐ b. Breedlove was careless when he prepared for his runs.

☐ c. Breedlove was not very skillful at handling his car.

4. The author probably wrote this article in order to

☐ a. share a humorous tale.

☐ b. persuade the reader to become a professional driver.

☐ c. describe the contributions of a daring individual.

_______ Number of correct answers

Record your personal assessment of your work on the Critical Thinking Chart on page 74.

Summarizing and Paraphrasing

Follow the directions provided for question 1. Put an X in the box next to the correct answer for the other questions.

1. Look for the important ideas and events in paragraphs 11 and 12. Summarize those paragraphs in one or two sentences.

____

____

____

2. Read the statement about the article below. Then read the paraphrase of that statement. Choose the reason that best tells why the paraphrase does not say the same thing as the statement.

Statement: Hit by crosswinds and buffeted by shock waves, Breedlove's car spun out of control.

Paraphrase: Breedlove lost control of his car.

☐ a. Paraphrase says too much.

☐ b. Paraphrase doesn't say enough.

☐ c. Paraphrase doesn't agree with the statement about the article.

3. Choose the best one-sentence paraphrase for the following sentence from the article:

"On September 26, 1997, Andy Green raised the bar again."

☐ a. On September 26, 1997, Andy Green became a high jumper, leaving the world of fast cars behind.

☐ b. On September 26, 1997, Andy Green opened the doors of his new bar and restaurant.

☐ c. On September 26, 1997, Andy Green set a new record—one that others would need to beat.

_______ Number of correct answers

Record your personal assessment of your work on the Critical Thinking Chart on page 74.

Critical Thinking

Follow the directions provided for questions 1 and 2. Put an X in the box next to the correct answer for questions 3 and 4.

1. For each statement below, write O if it expresses an opinion or write F if it expresses a fact.

_______ a. Craig Breedlove is one of the best drivers in the history of the world.

_______ b. Craig Breedlove was the first car driver to go 400 m.p.h.

_______ c. It's almost unbelievable that anyone could flip his car at 420 m.p.h. and walk away from the crash unhurt.

2. Choose from the letters below to correctly complete the following statement. Write the letters on the lines.

   On the positive side, _________, but on the negative side _________.

   a. Breedlove maintained his enthusiasm for speed for many years
   b. Breedlove's car was named *Spirit of America.*
   c. Breedlove failed to reach his final goal

3. What was the cause of Breedlove's accident in the Utah salt flats in 1964?

☐ a. Breedlove was thrown into a pond.
☐ b. Breedlove lost his parachutes and his brakes as he tried to slow down.
☐ c. Breedlove's car hit a telephone pole.

4. If you were a car driver trying to break records, how could you use the information in the article to reach your goals?

☐ a. You could find the addresses of the drivers mentioned in this article and write to them for advice.
☐ b. Using what you learned here, you could plan a car just like *Spirit of America.*
☐ c. Like Breedlove, you could give your car a name.

_________ Number of correct answers

Record your personal assessment of your work on the Critical Thinking Chart on page 71.

Personal Response

If you could ask the author of the article one question, what would it be?

____

____

____

____

Self-Assessment

A word or phrase in the article that I do not understand is

____

____

____

____

Compare and Contrast

Think about the articles you have read in Unit One. Pick the four daredevils that you admire the most. Write the titles of the articles about them in the first column of the chart below. Use information you learned from the articles to fill in the empty boxes in the chart.

Title	This daredevil risked his or her life. In your opinion, which outcomes (if any) justified that risk?	How did this daredevil prepare for his or her dangerous activity?	What qualities do you most admire in this person?

The daredevil who I thought was most courageous was ______________________________ because ______________________________

____

____

Words-per-Minute Table

Unit One

Directions: If you were timed while reading an article, refer to the Reading Time you recorded in the box at the end of the article. Use this words-per-minute table to determine your reading speed for that article. Then plot your reading speed on the graph on page 72.

Lesson	Sample	1	2	3	4	5	6	7	
No. of Words	939	991	1027	1006	1032	1147	1086	1276	*Seconds*
Minutes and Seconds									
1:30	626	661	685	671	688	765	724	851	**90**
1:40	563	595	616	604	619	688	652	766	**100**
1:50	512	541	560	549	563	626	592	696	**110**
2:00	470	496	514	503	516	574	543	638	**120**
2:10	433	457	474	464	476	529	501	589	**130**
2:20	402	425	440	431	442	492	465	547	**140**
2:30	376	396	411	402	413	459	434	510	**150**
2:40	352	372	385	377	387	430	407	479	**160**
2:50	331	350	362	355	364	405	383	450	**170**
3:00	313	330	342	335	344	382	362	425	**180**
3:10	297	313	324	318	326	362	343	403	**190**
3:20	282	297	308	302	310	344	326	383	**200**
3:30	268	283	293	287	295	328	310	365	**210**
3:40	256	270	280	274	281	313	296	348	**220**
3:50	245	259	268	262	269	299	283	333	**230**
4:00	235	248	257	252	258	287	272	319	**240**
4:10	225	238	246	241	248	275	261	306	**250**
4:20	217	229	237	232	238	265	251	294	**260**
4:30	209	220	228	224	229	255	241	284	**270**
4:40	201	212	220	216	221	246	233	273	**280**
4:50	194	205	212	208	214	237	225	264	**290**
5:00	188	198	205	201	206	229	217	255	**300**
5:10	182	192	199	195	200	222	210	247	**310**
5:20	176	186	193	189	194	215	204	239	**320**
5:30	171	180	187	183	188	209	197	232	**330**
5:40	166	175	181	178	182	202	192	225	**340**
5:50	161	170	176	172	177	197	186	219	**350**
6:00	157	165	171	168	172	191	181	213	**360**
6:10	152	161	167	163	167	186	176	207	**370**
6:20	148	156	162	159	163	181	171	201	**380**
6:30	144	152	158	155	159	176	167	196	**390**
6:40	141	149	154	151	155	172	163	191	**400**
6:50	137	145	150	147	151	168	159	187	**410**
7:00	134	142	147	144	147	164	155	182	**420**
7:10	131	138	143	140	144	160	152	178	**430**
7:20	128	135	140	137	141	156	148	174	**440**
7:30	125	132	137	134	138	153	145	170	**450**
7:40	122	129	134	131	135	150	142	166	**460**
7:50	120	127	131	128	132	146	139	163	**470**
8:00	117	124	128	126	129	143	136	160	**480**

Plotting Your Progress: Reading Speed

Unit One

Directions: If you were timed while reading an article, write your words-per-minute rate for that article in the box under the number of the lesson. Then plot your reading speed on the graph by putting a small X on the line directly above the number of the lesson, across from the number of words per minute you read. As you mark your speed for each lesson, graph your progress by drawing a line to connect the X's.

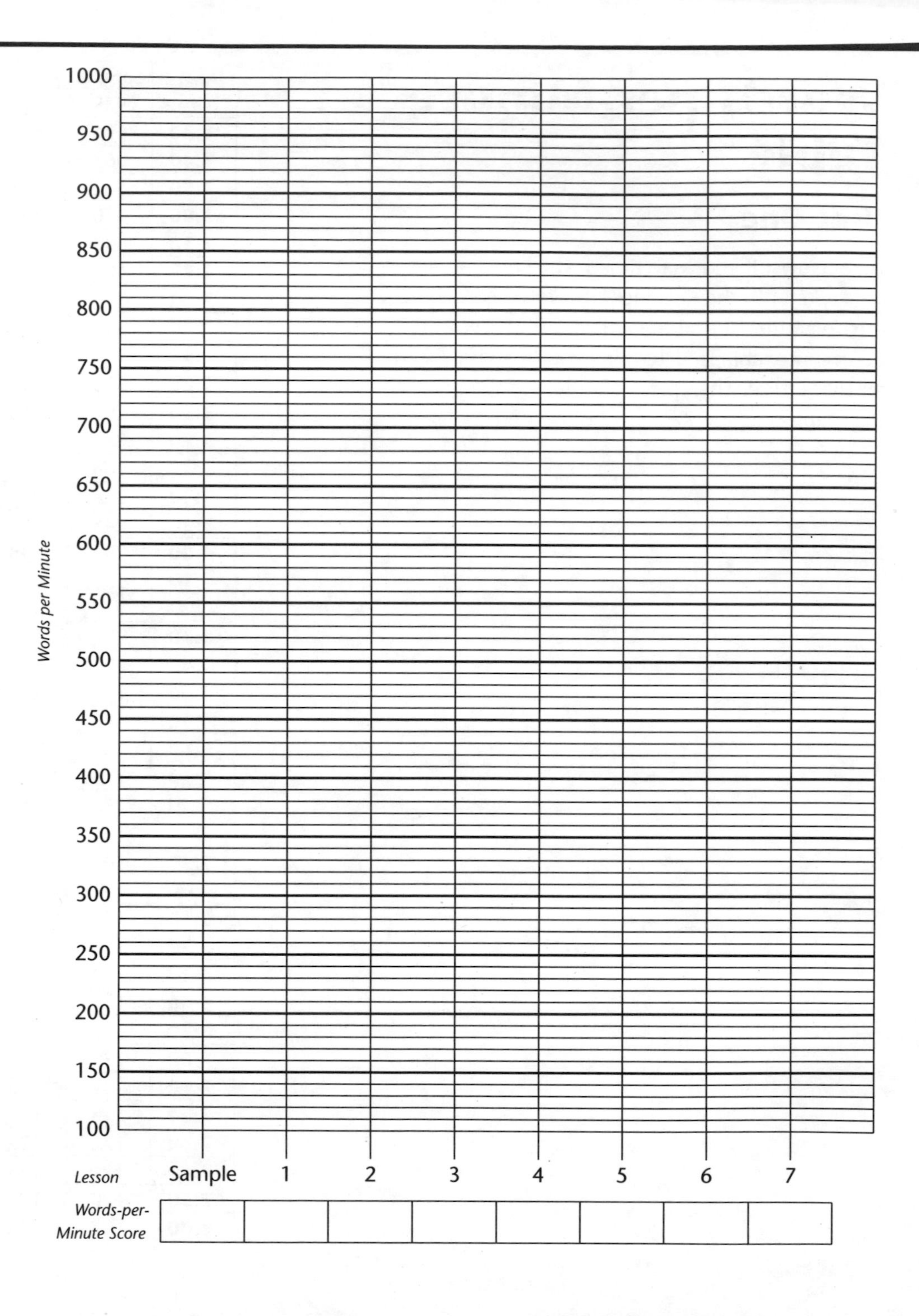

Plotting Your Progress: Reading Comprehension

Unit One

Directions: Write your Reading Comprehension score for each lesson in the box under the number of the lesson. Then plot your score on the graph by putting a small X on the line directly above the number of the lesson and across from the score you earned. As you mark your score for each lesson, graph your progress by drawing a line to connect the X's.

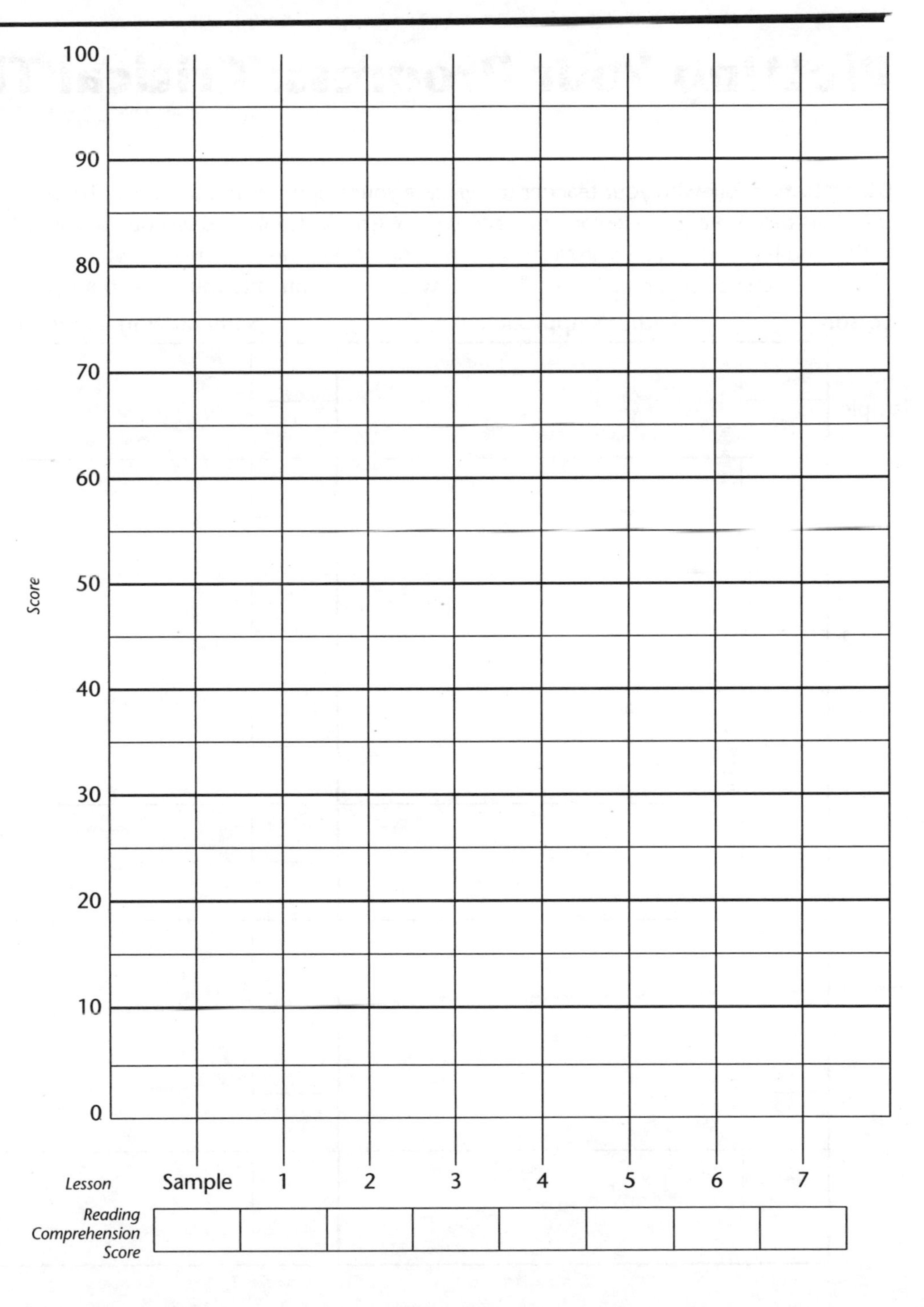

Plotting Your Progress: Critical Thinking

Unit One

Directions: Work with your teacher to evaluate your responses to the Critical Thinking questions for each lesson. Then fill in the appropriate spaces in the chart below. For each lesson and each type of Critical Thinking question, do the following: Mark a minus sign (–) in the box to indicate areas in which you feel you could improve. Mark a plus sign (+) to indicate areas in which you feel you did well. Mark a minus-slash-plus sign (–/+) to indicate areas in which you had mixed success. Then write any comments you have about your performance, including ideas for improvement.

Lesson	Author's Approach	Summarizing and Paraphrasing	Critical Thinking
Sample			
1			
2			
3			
4			
5			
6			
7			

UNIT TWO

THE GREAT WALLENDAS
Danger on the High Wire

Imagine walking across a three-quarter-inch steel wire that is 40 feet above the ground. You have ballet slippers on your feet and a balancing pole in your hands. Walking across that wire takes a huge amount of courage, even with a safety net. It's the kind of high-wire act that has long thrilled circus audiences.

2 Now imagine this. There is not just one person walking across the wire; there are three. They move in unison, with two men carrying another man on their shoulders. This "pyramid" act was invented in 1925 by a German circus performer named Karl Wallenda. Karl was the leader of a troupe known as the Great Wallendas.

3 In 1928, when he performed the pyramid stunt in New York City for the first time, Karl Wallenda wanted to make sure people loved it. So the day before his New York debut, Wallenda announced that the troupe would do its act the next day *without a net*. No one in the history of the American circus had ever done a pyramid on a high-wire. To do it without a net was sheer lunacy. Even so, the Wallendas pulled it off. When the audience saw the stunt, they cheered for 15 minutes straight.

The Flying Wallendas perform their seven-person Grand Pyramid in 1998.

[4] Karl Wallenda was always looking for ways to improve his act. In 1947, he invented an incredible seven-person pyramid. In his new act, four men walked on the wire. They were connected by steel rods fitted to shoulder harnesses. Two more men stood on these rods, forming a second tier. They, too, were yoked by a steel rod fitted to shoulder harnesses. On the third tier rode the seventh member—a woman perched high on a chair. Her chair rested on the rod that connected the men directly below her. The seven-person pyramid—performed without a net—may have been the most outrageous and dangerous circus stunt of all time.

[5] The members of the Great Wallendas constantly changed. But they were all part of the extended family—uncles, nieces, brothers, in-laws, and so forth. For example, Karl's wife, Helen, was once part of the act. She quit twice and threatened to quit hundreds of times. She couldn't stand working without a net. But Karl used his charm to talk her back onto the wire. In 1960, however, Helen quit for good.

[6] It was lucky for her that she did. Tragedy finally hit the Great Wallendas on January 30, 1962. The troupe was performing at the Shrine Circus in Detroit. More than 6,500 fans packed the State Fair Coliseum. The drums rolled, the arena darkened, and a thin blue spotlight picked up the Great Wallendas. At the high point of their act, they slowly inched out on the high wire in their famous seven-person pyramid.

[7] Dieter Schepp, a nephew of Karl Wallenda, led the way. It was the first time he had performed in public with the Great Wallendas. Jenny Wallenda Faughnan was standing on a platform at the end of the wire. She could see Schepp was in trouble. "He was holding [his balancing pole] with the tips of his fingers instead of the palms of his hand," she said. "He was getting tired. I saw him toss the pole into the air slightly to get a better grip. When he did that, he lost his balance."

[8] Schepp cried out, "I can't hold on anymore! I can't hold on anymore!"

[9] With that, the whole pyramid collapsed. Schepp was killed as he tumbled to the ground 40 feet below. Richard Faughnan also died, and Mario Wallenda was permanently paralyzed below the waist. Somehow, the others managed to grab hold of the wire and wrap their legs around it to save their lives.

[10] Only a miracle saved Jana Schepp, Richard's wife, who was riding in the chair. As Jana plunged toward the ground and almost certain death, Karl Wallenda reached out and grabbed her arm. Gunther Wallenda then grabbed her other arm. Circus workers below used a

Karl Wallenda, patriarch of the famous Flying Wallendas, loses his balance and falls to his death in San Juan, Puerto Rico, in 1978.

tumbling mat to catch Jana when the two men let her go. Still, she suffered a concussion when she bounced off the mat and hit her head on the concrete floor. The three men still on the wire managed to drag themselves to the safety of the platform. "It was like a nightmare," said Karl later. "I still can't believe it."

11 The Great Wallendas lived by their own special motto: "Life is on the wire; the rest is just waiting." Doing daredevil high-wire stunts was the heart and soul of their lives. So, despite the death of the two family members, the Great Wallendas performed the very next night. Instead of the seven-person stunt, they did a three-man pyramid. The sold-out crowd roared its approval. Still, Gunther Wallenda had a rare moment of doubt. "Yes, the show must go on," he said. "But every once in a while, you get to thinking—why?"

12 The seven-person pyramid was dropped from the act after the accident. But Karl Wallenda went on performing death-defying high wire stunts. Many times he worked alone. At the age of 66, he walked over Georgia's Tallulah Gorge, 750 feet in the air. A year later, he did a 640-foot walk across a stadium in Philadelphia. His walk that day thrilled the crowd. He even did a headstand on the wire halfway across. However his wife Helen refused to watch him. "I always sit in a back room and pray," she said.

13 On March 23, 1978, Karl Wallenda tried to walk on a wire between two hotels in Puerto Rico. He was 73 years old at the time. Still, for him, it was not a hard stunt. The planned walk was 100 feet above Ashford Avenue. Officials tried to warn him that the winds could be gusty. "Don't worry about it," said Karl. "The wind is stronger on the street than up here."

14 Karl Wallenda would not be stopped. He was fearless. And he put his destiny squarely in the hands of God. Karl once said, "God gives us the courage and the gift of talent to do our acts, and when he [is] ready to take us, he will."

15 That day, as Karl inched out on the wire, a gust of wind blew. The wire vibrated as he steadied himself. Just after Karl passed the halfway point, the cable began to sway. Again, he started to wobble. His young granddaughter, who was waiting on a hotel roof, saw the danger. She shouted, "Sit down, Poppy, sit down."

16 It was too late. Karl crouched down to regain his balance, but he fell anyway. As he had done 16 years earlier in Detroit, Karl grabbed the wire. But this time he couldn't hold on. He fell toward the street below, bounced off the roof of a taxi, and landed on the pavement. He died from massive internal injuries. After 57 years of high wire stunts, the greatest of the Great Wallendas had given his last performance.

If you have been timed while reading this article, enter your reading time below. Then turn to the Words-per-Minute Table on page 133 and look up your reading speed (words per minute). Enter your reading speed on the graph on page 134.

Reading Time: Lesson 8

________ : ________

Minutes *Seconds*

A Finding the Main Idea

One statement below expresses the main idea of the article. One statement is too general, or too broad. The other statement explains only part of the article; it is too narrow. Label the statements using the following key:

M—Main Idea **B—Too Broad** **N—Too Narrow**

_______ 1. The seven-person pyramid was the act for which the Wallenda family was best known.

_______ 2. Karl Wallenda, along with other family members, successfully performed death-defying stunts on the high wire, but some family members paid the ultimate price.

_______ 3. For some people, such as high-wire walkers, danger is the spice of life.

_______ Score 15 points for a correct M answer.

_______ Score 5 points for each correct B or N answer.

_______ **Total Score:** Finding the Main Idea

B Recalling Facts

How well do you remember the facts in the article? Put an X in the box next to the answer that correctly completes each statement about the article.

1. After its debut in New York, the pyramid act was performed
- ☐ a. without a net.
- ☐ b. every day.
- ☐ c. only once.

2. On the top level of the seven-person pyramid was a
- ☐ a. family member on a bicycle.
- ☐ b. man doing a headstand.
- ☐ c. woman on a chair.

3. The seven-person pyramid fell when the troupe was playing
- ☐ a. New York City.
- ☐ b. Detroit.
- ☐ c. Germany.

4. After she quit the act, Helen always
- ☐ a. watched Karl's act from below.
- ☐ b. refused to watch Karl's act.
- ☐ c. stood at the side of the wire, ready to help.

5. Karl Wallenda died while trying to walk a wire
- ☐ a. over a stadium in Philadelphia.
- ☐ b. over the Tallulah Gorge in Georgia.
- ☐ c. between two hotels in Puerto Rico.

Score 5 points for each correct answer.

_______ **Total Score:** Recalling Facts

C Making Inferences

When you combine your own experience and information from a text to draw a conclusion that is not directly stated in that text, you are making an inference. Below are five statements that may or may not be inferences based on information in the article. Label the statements using the following key:

C—Correct Inference **F—Faulty Inference**

_______ 1. Karl Wallenda was pleased when members of his family agreed to join his act.

_______ 2. The Wallendas practiced their act regularly.

_______ 3. The men at the bottom of the pyramid played the most important role in making the act work successfully.

_______ 4. Karl Wallenda was both stubborn and brave.

_______ 5. After the pyramid accident, Karl Wallenda refused to work with other family members.

Score 5 points for each correct answer.

_______ **Total Score:** Making Inferences

D Using Words Precisely

Each numbered sentence below contains an underlined word or phrase from the article. Following the sentence are three definitions. One definition is closest to the meaning of the underlined word. One definition is opposite or nearly opposite. Label those two definitions using the following key. Do not label the remaining definition.

C—Closest **O—Opposite or Nearly Opposite**

1. They move in unison, with two men carrying another man on their shoulders

_______ a. skillfully

_______ b. together

_______ c. separately

2. To do it without a net was sheer lunacy.

_______ a. madness

_______ b. good sense

_______ c. entertainment

3. They, too, were yoked by a steel rod fitted to shoulder harnesses.

_______ a. separated

_______ b. injured

_______ c. joined

4. With that, the whole pyramid collapsed.

_______ a. united strongly

_______ b. fell apart

_______ c. quivered

5. The wire vibrated as he steadied himself.

a. stayed motionless

b. whined

c. moved up and down, or from side to side

_______ Score 3 points for each correct C answer.

_______ Score 2 points for each correct O answer.

_______ **Total Score:** Using Words Precisely

Enter the four total scores in the spaces below, and add them together to find your Reading Comprehension Score. Then record your score on the graph on page 135.

Score	Question Type	Lesson 8
_______	Finding the Main Idea	
_______	Recalling Facts	
_______	Making Inferences	
_______	Using Words Precisely	
_______	**Reading Comprehension Score**	

Author's Approach

Put an X in the box next to the correct answer.

1. The main purpose of the first paragraph is to

☐ a. help the reader imagine what it feels like to walk on the high wire.

☐ b. inform the reader about the life of Karl Wallenda.

☐ c. encourage the reader to try to walk the high wire.

2. Which of the following statements from the article best describes Helen Wallenda's attitude toward her own performance in the high-wire act?

☐ a. "For example, Karl's wife, Helen, was once part of the act."

☐ b. "However, his wife Helen refused to watch him."

☐ c. "She couldn't stand working without a net."

3. Judging by statements from the article "The Great Wallendas: Danger on the High Wire," you can conclude that the author wants the reader to think that

☐ a. many members of the Wallenda family wanted to join Karl in his high-wire act.

☐ b. Karl Wallenda forced the members of his family to join him.

☐ c. all the members of the Wallenda family loved walking the wire.

4. The author tells this story mainly by

☐ a. telling about events in the order they happened.

☐ b. comparing different topics.

☐ c. using his or her imagination and creativity.

_______ Number of correct answers

Record your personal assessment of your work on the Critical Thinking Chart on page 136.

Summarizing and Paraphrasing

Follow the directions provided for questions 1 and 2.

1. Complete the following one-sentence summary of the article using the lettered phrases from the phrase bank below. Write the letters on the lines.

Phrase Bank:

a. the seven-person pyramid and the terrible accident
b. the early years of the Wallenda act
c. the death of Karl Wallenda

After a short introduction, the article about the Great Wallendas begins with________, goes on to explain________, and ends with________.

2. Reread paragraph 10 in the article. Below, write a summary of the paragraph in no more than 25 words.

____

____

____

____

Reread your summary and decide whether it covers the important ideas in the paragraph. Next, decide how to shorten the summary to 15 words or less without leaving out any essential information. Write this summary below.

____

____

____

________ Number of correct answers

Record your personal assessment of your work on the Critical Thinking Chart on page 136.

Critical Thinking

Put an X in the box next to the correct answer for questions 1, 2, and 4. Follow the directions provided for questions 3 and 5.

1. Which of the following statements from the article is an opinion rather than a fact?

☐ a. "The seven-person pyramid—performed without a net—may have been the most outrageous and dangerous circus stunt of all time."

☐ b. "The members of the Great Wallendas constantly changed."

☐ c. "On March 23, 1978, Karl Wallenda tried to walk on a wire between two hotels in Puerto Rico."

2. From what the article told about Karl Wallenda, you can predict that if he were alive today, he would

- ☐ a. have no interest in any high-wire acts anymore.
- ☐ b. regret ever having walked on the high wire.
- ☐ c. still be willing to try to walk the high wire.

3. Choose from the letters below to correctly complete the following statement. Write the letters on the lines.

In the article, ________ and ________ are different in their determination to keep the high-wire act going.

a. Helen Wallenda
b. Karl Wallenda
c. Gunther Wallenda

4. What was the cause of the collapse of the seven-person pyramid in 1962?

- ☐ a. A gust of wind shook the high wire.
- ☐ b. Dieter Schepp lost his balance.
- ☐ c. The chair fell off the top of the pyramid.

5. Which paragraphs from the article provide evidence that supports your answer to question 4?

____

________ Number of correct answers

Record your personal assessment of your work on the Critical Thinking Chart on page 136.

Personal Response

Why do you think Karl Wallenda continued to walk the high wire in spite of its risks?

____

____

____

____

Self-Assessment

I can't really understand how

____

____

____

____

MARY KINGSLEY
Explorer

One day Mary Kingsley decided to take a shortcut through the dense African bush. That wasn't a good idea. Without warning, the ground suddenly gave way under her feet and she tumbled 15 feet straight down into a game trap. Local hunters had lined the bottom of the pit with nine-foot-long spikes. Kingsley survived with only bruises because she was wearing a thick woolen skirt. Otherwise, as she wrote in 1897, "I should have been spiked to the bone and done for."

2 What was Kingsley doing in Africa? Today her travels would be no big deal. Many modern women head off around the world in search of adventure. But in the 19th century, such boldness was shocking. Other people's expectations, however, did not stop Kingsley. She went exploring in Africa three times between 1893 and 1900. Her daring and courage rivaled those of such famous male explorers as Richard Burton and Henry Morton Stanley. Rudyard Kipling, the famous writer, knew Kingsley. "Being human, she must have been afraid of

Explorer Mary Kingsley in her canoe on the Ogowe River in Gabon in 1896. Inset: Portrait of Mary Kingsley.

something," he said, "but no one ever found out what it was."

3 Mary Kingsley was born in England in 1862. The first 30 years of her life were anything but exciting. Like many other girls at this time, she did not go to school. Still, she was not uneducated. She learned by reading books and listening to family conversations. Although her father was trained as a doctor, his true passion was anthropology. He roamed the world to study native cultures from the South Seas to the American Rockies to West Africa. One of Mary Kingsley's uncles was a sea captain. Another was a well-known English novelist.

4 Such role models must have fired her imagination. Yet, even as a young adult she rarely left the house. She spent most of her time inside doing housework and tending to her sick mother. Later her father, too, became an invalid. As a dutiful daughter, Kingsley nursed both her parents. In her spare time, she prepared her father's notes on sacrificial rites in West Africa for publication. In 1892, her parents died within six weeks of each other.

5 Suddenly free from family obligations, Kingsley did not waste any time. She sold the family house and made plans to go to Africa. She wanted to see for herself what she had only heard her father talk about or had read about in books. Kingsley's goal was to investigate fish species and native customs of West Africa. She would go to parts of Africa where no white person had ever gone before. What's more, she would do it with only a few African guides.

6 Kingsley made two trips to West Africa. In 1893, she stayed for six months. Then, in 1895, she returned and remained for nearly a year. During those fairly brief excursions, she saw and did more than most people do in a lifetime. She collected insects and found new species of fish, three of which were named for her. She taught herself how to canoe through rapids. She explored mysterious bogs and jungles. And despite the intense heat of West Africa, she always dressed as a proper English lady. She wore a white blouse and a long black woolen skirt.

7 Mary Kingsley never used her gender as an excuse. If a man could do something, so could she—and she could

This small village in the mountains of Cameroon shows that in some areas life has not changed much since the days of Mary Kingsley's explorations.

usually do it better. Richard Burton once climbed to the 13,760-foot summit of Mount Cameroon. A couple of other men had also climbed it. But they all took the easy western route. Kingsley chose the much more difficult southeast route and she did it in bad weather.

8 Kingsley's polite manner disarmed all those she met. She would pop up in the weirdest places and say, "It's only me." On the ship to Africa, passengers were not supposed to go into the engine room or the bridge. That didn't stop the ever-curious Kingsley from inspecting both. In West Africa, she would show up at a trading village or a native gathering and simply announce, "It's only me." Kingsley said those words so often some Africans thought her name was "only me."

9 Naturally, Africans were fascinated by her. Many had seen a few white men before, but none had ever seen a white woman. Children, she reported, often rolled in the street and howled in shock at the sight of her. But since she came only to study and to trade, village elders treated her with kindness.

10 At one point, Kingsley visited the Fang people of Gabon. They were feared throughout West Africa for their ferocity. Totally unafraid, Kingsley went to visit them because she wanted to study their customs. She won their trust by her gentle behavior. One night, the Fang chief honored Kingsley by letting her stay in his hut. Soon, however, she noticed a strange odor. She found the source—some small bags. "I took down the biggest one," she later wrote. "I then shook its contents out in my hat, for fear of losing anything of value. They were a human hand, three big toes, four eyes, two ears, and other portions of the human body."

11 Although she often suffered from malaria, Kingsley loved every minute in Africa. Lying ill on the floor of a mud hut or in the damp bottom of a canoe was all part of the experience. "Skylarking" or "stalking Africa" was what she called it. Her adventures, she wrote, "took all the color out of other kinds of living."

12 In 1897, Kingsley published her memoirs, *Travels in West Africa*. She left out some of her wilder exploits because she didn't want to overdo it. If she told the whole truth, she felt, some people would reject the book as a pack of lies. But in her lectures, she told some of these other tales. Once, for example, a Fang guide shot a gorilla just as it was about to kill her. Another time, a crocodile climbed into her canoe. She had to beat it off with her paddle.

13 In 1899, Kingsley planned to go back to West Africa, but the Boer War broke out in South Africa. England was at war with the Dutch settlers, known as Boers. Kingsley felt it was her duty to help with the war effort. She reached South Africa in 1900. There she nursed wounded Boer prisoners in a makeshift hospital. It was not a pleasant task. "All this work here," she wrote, "the stench, the washing...the bed pans, the blood, is my world."

14 Many of the prisoners died of enteric fever. Kingsley soon got the fever, too. She died within three months, on June 3, 1900. By her own request, she was buried at sea the following day. Mary Kingsley was just 37 years old. But what a life she had packed into those last seven years!

If you have been timed while reading this article, enter your reading time below. Then turn to the Words-per-Minute Table on page 133 and look up your reading speed (words per minute). Enter your reading speed on the graph on page 134.

Reading Time: Lesson 9

_______ : _______

Minutes *Seconds*

A Finding the Main Idea

One statement below expresses the main idea of the article. One statement is too general, or too broad. The other statement explains only part of the article; it is too narrow. Label the statements using the following key:

M—Main Idea **B—Too Broad** **N—Too Narrow**

_____ 1. In 1897, explorer Mary Kingsley wrote a book that described many of her exciting adventures in Africa.

_____ 2. Exploring the African bush can be dangerous for anyone, but it is especially risky for an inexperienced, would-be explorer.

_____ 3. Daredevil Mary Kingsley performed dangerous investigations while on her trips to Africa during the 19th century.

_____ Score 15 points for a correct M answer.

_____ Score 5 points for each correct B or N answer.

_____ **Total Score:** Finding the Main Idea

B Recalling Facts

How well do you remember the facts in the article? Put an X in the box next to the answer that correctly completes each statement about the article.

1. People were surprised that Mary Kingsley wanted to explore Africa because she was
- ☐ a. from England.
- ☐ b. rich.
- ☐ c. a woman.

2. One of Kingsley's main goals in going to Africa the first time was to
- ☐ a. find new plants.
- ☐ b. investigate fish species.
- ☐ c. report on the activities of other explorers.

3. While in Africa, Kingsley wore
- ☐ a. a white blouse and a long black woolen skirt.
- ☐ b. a white blouse and black woolen pants.
- ☐ c. a khaki-colored uniform.

4. Off and on, Kingsley suffered from
- ☐ a. pneumonia.
- ☐ b. malaria.
- ☐ c. heart disease.

5. In 1900, Kingsley was not able to explore Africa as she had planned because
- ☐ a. African natives would not allow her in their countries anymore.
- ☐ b. English officials would not allow any travel to Africa.
- ☐ c. she decided to help in a Boer prisoner hospital instead.

Score 5 points for each correct answer.

_____ **Total Score:** Recalling Facts

C Making Inferences

When you combine your own experience and information from a text to draw a conclusion that is not directly stated in that text, you are making an inference. Below are five statements that may or may not be inferences based on information in the article. Label the statements using the following key:

C—Correct Inference **F—Faulty Inference**

_______ 1. Mary Kingsley resented having to stay home and care for her parents.

_______ 2. Kingsley felt it was important to dress as an English lady at all times.

_______ 3. Many people in England were fascinated by Kingsley's stories of adventure in Africa.

_______ 4. Kingsley's African guides probably helped her survive many difficult situations.

_______ 5. Kingsley was the only woman who ever explored Africa.

Score 5 points for each correct answer.

_______ **Total Score:** Making Inferences

D Using Words Precisely

Each numbered sentence below contains an underlined word or phrase from the article. Following the sentence are three definitions. One definition is closest to the meaning of the underlined word. One definition is opposite or nearly opposite. Label those two definitions using the following key. Do not label the remaining definition.

C—Closest **O—Opposite or Nearly Opposite**

1. Her daring and courage rivaled those of such famous male explorers as Richard Burton and Henry Morton Stanley.

_______ a. ridiculed

_______ b. were nothing like

_______ c. were a close match for

2. Such role models must have fired her imagination.

_______ a. given life to

_______ b. trusted

_______ c. killed

3. Later her father, too, became an invalid.

_______ a. person who eats too much

_______ b. person in good health

_______ c. sick person

4. Kingsley's polite manner disarmed all those she met.

_______ a. made harmless

_______ b. made violent

_______ c. shocked

5. They were feared throughout West Africa for their ferocity.

_______ a. ugliness

_______ b. fierceness and cruelty

_______ c. gentleness

_______ Score 3 points for each correct C answer.

_______ Score 2 points for each correct O answer.

_______ **Total Score:** Using Words Precisely

Enter the four total scores in the spaces below, and add them together to find your Reading Comprehension Score. Then record your score on the graph on page 135.

Score	Question Type	Lesson 9
_______	Finding the Main Idea	
_______	Recalling Facts	
_______	Making Inferences	
_______	Using Words Precisely	
_______	**Reading Comprehension Score**	

Author's Approach

Put an X in the box next to the correct answer.

1. What is the author's purpose in writing "Mary Kingsley: Explorer"?

☐ a. To encourage the reader to become an explorer like Kingsley

☐ b. To express an opinion about life in 19th century England

☐ c. To inform the reader about a brave adventurer

2. Judging by statements from the article "Mary Kingsley: Explorer," you can conclude that the author wants the reader to think that

☐ a. most women in 19th century England had limited opportunities.

☐ b. most women in 19th century were happy with the limitations society put on them.

☐ c. modern women have no limitations on what they can or cannot do.

3. What does the author imply by saying "She would pop up in the weirdest places and say, 'It's only me'"?

☐ a. Kingsley acted shy when she met new people.

☐ b. Kingsley had no self confidence.

☐ c. Kingsley was not a proud or haughty woman.

4. Choose the statement below that best describes the author's position in paragraph 14.

☐ a. Mary Kingsley was a strange person.

☐ b. Mary Kingsley lived life to the fullest.

☐ c. Mary Kingsley had foolishly wasted her life.

_______ Number of correct answers

Record your personal assessment of your work on the Critical Thinking Chart on page 136.

Summarizing and Paraphrasing

Put an X in the box next to the correct answer.

1. Below are summaries of the article. Choose the summary that says all the most important things about the article but in the fewest words.

☐ a. Mary Kingsley was among the few people daring enough to explore the African continent.

☐ b. Ignoring 19th century society's expectations of her as a proper English lady, Mary Kingsley explored Africa, facing dangers bravely.

☐ c. Even when explorer Mary Kingsley was in danger or ill, she maintained her optimistic attitude toward life; in fact, she called her adventures "skylarking."

2. Choose the sentence that correctly restates the following sentence from the article:

"Her adventures, she wrote, 'took all the color out of other kinds of living.'"

☐ a. She wrote that her adventures made other ways of life seem boring.

☐ b. She wrote that her adventures made her forget her life in England.

☐ c. She wrote that her adventures destroyed other ways of life.

_______ Number of correct answers

Record your personal assessment of your work on the Critical Thinking Chart on page 136.

Critical Thinking

Follow the directions provided for questions 1, 2, and 3. Put an X in the box next to the correct answer for question 4.

1. For each statement below, write O if it expresses an opinion or write F if it expresses a fact.

_______ a. Mary Kingsley died of enteric fever at the age of 37.

_______ b. After her parents died, Kingsley sold the family home and set off for Africa.

_______ c. Kingsley should be honored as one of the great explorers of the 19th century.

2. Choose from the letters below to correctly complete the following statement. Write the letters on the lines.

On the positive side, _______, but on the negative side _______.

a. Kingsley died an early death, at the age of 37

b. Kingsley enjoyed her life immensely during her final years

c. Kingsley gave lectures about her adventures

3. Choose from the letters below to correctly complete the following statement. Write the letters on the lines.

According to the article, _______ caused Kingsley to _______, and the effect was _______.

a. Kingsley explored Africa and wrote about the people she met there

b. Kingsley's father's passion for anthropology

c. become interested in studying different cultures

4. Of the following theme categories, which would this story fit into?

☐ a. Don't rock the boat.

☐ b. Follow your dreams and you will be happy.

☐ c. There's no place like home.

_______ Number of correct answers

Record your personal assessment of your work on the Critical Thinking Chart on page 136.

Personal Response

What new question do you have about this topic?

____

____

____

____

Self-Assessment

I can't really understand how

____

____

____

____

MARIO ANDRETTI
Racing Legend

The 53rd annual Indianapolis 500 on May 30, 1969, begins with Mario Andretti (center car) as one of the three leaders.

What makes someone climb into a car and race around a track at speeds of up to 200 miles per hour? What makes drivers risk death in an effort to edge out other racers? If anyone could answer that question, it would be Mario Andretti. For over 30 years, Mario was the biggest name in auto racing.

2 Not only did Mario Andretti drive fast, but he drove fast in all kinds of cars in all kinds of races. Most race car drivers specialize. They drive either stock cars or Indy cars or Formula One cars. But Mario raced them all and won with them all. He is the only race car driver ever to win top races in the three main classes. He drove a stock car to win the Daytona 500 in 1967. He drove an Indy car to take the Indianapolis 500 race in 1969. And he won the world championship in Formula One Grand Prix racing in 1978.

3 Mario fell in love with auto racing as a child growing up in Italy. An uncle once took him and his twin brother, Aldo, to see a 1,000-mile cross-country car race. "It just caught my fancy," Mario recalled. "I

just became totally fascinated. That was something I wanted to pursue in life."

4 At the age of 13, Mario and Aldo joined a driving program. Its purpose was to train young race car drivers. The two boys won a few races, but the program was soon canceled. "Lots of kids got hurt and some got killed," said Mario. "And that ended it." Feeling the sport was too dangerous, Mario's father opposed any more racing by his sons. But secretly, both boys continued to race anyway.

5 In 1955, the Andretti family moved to the United States. Mario took a job as a welder in a garage. He and Aldo saved their money. Before long, they had enough cash to buy an old Hudson Hornet car. Still keeping the secret from their father, they rebuilt the car and took turns racing it. Mario alone won more than 20 stock car races. They got away with their clandestine racing for three years. But then, in 1959, Aldo was badly injured in a race accident. Mario's father was not happy when he found out about the deception. Once again, he demanded that his boys give up racing. But Mario's love of racing was too great. Rather than give up the sport he loved, he ran away from home. Realizing that nothing could stop Mario from racing, Mr. Andretti soon gave up and began to support his son's endeavors.

6 In 1961, Mario quit his job at the garage and took up racing full time. At first, he raced small cars on a minor league circuit. He won many races but needed a sponsor to join the big leagues of auto racing. Sponsors pay for the car, the pit crew, and the equipment. Most sponsors were not interested in Mario. They thought he was too reckless; they feared he would ruin too many cars. Clint Brawner, however, liked what he saw in the young man. Brawner talked Dean Van Lines into sponsoring Mario. It wasn't a mistake.

7 In 1965, Mario won the national driving championship. He bested such famous drivers as A. J. Foyt and Parnelli Jones. The title was based on a point system. Although Mario won only one race, he had enough second and third place finishes to win. Still, he didn't impress some of the old pros. Foyt would have won the championship had he not run out of gas on the last lap of the Indianapolis 500. "We'll have to wait and see how good he really is," said Foyt at the time.

8 The racing world didn't have to wait long. Mario Andretti won the championship again in 1966. This time there were no doubts, no second-guessers. Mario entered 15 major races, winning eight of them. In three straight races, he led from start to finish. No one had ever done that before. Now even Foyt had to admit that Mario was "the one to beat."

9 That situation remained unchanged for the next 30 years. Mario was the dominant driver on any kind of track in any kind of car. He was the superstar of auto racing. Even people with no interest in racing could name one driver—Mario Andretti.

Badly burned in a race only a week earlier, Mario Andretti wins the 53rd Indianapolis 500 in a record time of 3 hours, 11 minutes and 14.71 seconds.

10 Mario raced in his final Indy 500 in 1994. By then he'd had his share of accidents. He had smacked into more walls than he could remember. Once, in 1966, he was in a tragic crash that killed four spectators. Luckily for Andretti, his own injuries were mostly minor—cracked ribs and bruises. Mario never liked to think about the risks he took in all those races. "When you start thinking you may get hurt," said Mario, "it's time to get out of racing."

11 Mario was fortunate to have survived so long in such a dangerous sport. But it wasn't all luck. Skill played a large part as well. Take the 1985 Indy 500, for example. On lap 120, Danny Sullivan's car spun out of control. Sullivan did a 360-degree turn but didn't hit anything. Still, he ended up right in Mario's path. Mario's car was bearing down on him. At the last instant, Mario swerved down onto the infield grass to avoid Sullivan. It was one of the greatest moves ever seen at Indy. Quite possibly, Mario saved Sullivan's life. The move also allowed Sullivan to recover and win the race. "It was his day," said Mario. "I can't explain these things."

12 Given all the things that could—and did—go wrong from time to time, why did Mario choose to make a career out of auto racing? In 1997, a reporter asked him that very question. "What makes you do it?" asked the newsman. "Is it a controlled terror? Is there a fear there that you just have to take control of? Or is it an adrenaline rush and it's just fun?"

13 Mario Andretti answered the question with a laugh. "Well," he said, "all of the above."

14 But although Mario spent a good part of his life driving cars 150 to 200 miles per hour, he said he never went over the speed limit when driving the family car around town. When not on the track, he said, "I'm driving like a grandmother." After a short pause, he added, "Grandmother, I think she drives faster than I do."

If you have been timed while reading this article, enter your reading time below. Then turn to the Words-per-Minute Table on page 133 and look up your reading speed (words per minute). Enter your reading speed on the graph on page 134.

Reading Time: Lesson 10

_______ : _______

Minutes *Seconds*

A Finding the Main Idea

One statement below expresses the main idea of the article. One statement is too general, or too broad. The other statement explains only part of the article; it is too narrow. Label the statements using the following key:

M—Main Idea **B—Too Broad** **N—Too Narrow**

_______ 1. For years, Mario Andretti dominated the world of car racing.

_______ 2. Mario Andretti won the Daytona 500 in 1967.

_______ 3. Racing fans are all familiar with the name Mario Andretti.

_______ Score 15 points for a correct M answer.

_______ Score 5 points for each correct B or N answer.

_______ **Total Score:** Finding the Main Idea

B Recalling Facts

How well do you remember the facts in the article? Put an X in the box next to the answer that correctly completes each statement about the article.

1. Andretti saw his first car race as a boy in
- ☐ a. Italy.
- ☐ b. Indiana.
- ☐ c. Paris.

2. In the beginning, most sponsors avoided Andretti because he was too
- ☐ a. young.
- ☐ b. reckless.
- ☐ c. poor.

3. The national driving championship is given to whoever wins the
- ☐ a. Formula One Grand Prix.
- ☐ b. Indy 500.
- ☐ c. most points in a series of races.

4. Andretti raced his final Indy 500 in
- ☐ a. 1994.
- ☐ b. 1975.
- ☐ c. 1948.

5. In the 1985 Indy 500, Andretti swerved to avoid
- ☐ a. a pedestrian crossing the track.
- ☐ b. the pace car.
- ☐ c. a race car that had gone out of control.

Score 5 points for each correct answer.

_______ **Total Score:** Recalling Facts

C Making Inferences

When you combine your own experience and information from a text to draw a conclusion that is not directly stated in that text, you are making an inference. Below are five statements that may or may not be inferences based on information in the article. Label the statements using the following key:

C—Correct Inference **F—Faulty Inference**

_______ 1. Andretti's father always knew where his sons were.

_______ 2. Mario and Aldo were not only brothers but also good friends.

_______ 3. Sponsors don't care how much money they have to spend to make their drivers competitive.

_______ 4. A. J. Foyt felt that Andretti never deserved the attention he got from fans.

_______ 5. Danny Sullivan was glad that Andretti was such a skillful driver.

Score 5 points for each correct answer.

_______ **Total Score:** Making Inferences

D Using Words Precisely

Each numbered sentence below contains an underlined word or phrase from the article. Following the sentence are three definitions. One definition is closest to the meaning of the underlined word. One definition is opposite or nearly opposite. Label those two definitions using the following key. Do not label the remaining definition.

C—Closest **O—Opposite or Nearly Opposite**

1. Most race car drivers <u>specialize</u>.

_______ a. work in a variety of fields

_______ b. concentrate on a specific area or skill

_______ c. are extraordinary

2. They got away with their <u>clandestine</u> racing for three years.

_______ a. out in the open

_______ b. illegal

_______ c. secret

3. He <u>bested</u> such famous drivers as A. J. Foyt and Parnelli Jones.

_______ a. outdid

_______ b. admired

_______ c. was defeated by

4. Mario was the <u>dominant</u> driver on any kind of track in any kind of car.

_______ a. youngest

_______ b. leading

_______ c. least powerful

5. At the last instant, Mario <u>swerved</u> down onto the infield grass to avoid Sullivan.

_______ a. turned aside

_______ b. looked

_______ c. moved in a straight line

_______ Score 3 points for each correct C answer.

_______ Score 2 points for each correct O answer.

_______ **Total Score:** Using Words Precisely

Enter the four total scores in the spaces below, and add them together to find your Reading Comprehension Score. Then record your score on the graph on page 135.

Score	Question Type	Lesson 10
_______	Finding the Main Idea	
_______	Recalling Facts	
_______	Making Inferences	
_______	Using Words Precisely	
_______	**Reading Comprehension Score**	

Author's Approach

Put an X in the box next to the correct answer.

1. The main purpose of the first paragraph is to

☐ a. criticize Mario Andretti for participating in such a dangerous sport.

☐ b. compare auto racing and horseracing.

☐ c. introduce the reader to Mario Andretti and to identify his profession.

2. Which of the following statements from the article best describes Andretti's feelings about car racing?

☐ a. "At age 13, Mario and Aldo joined a driving program."

☐ b. "Mario fell in love with auto racing as a child growing up in Italy."

☐ c. "Mario was the dominant driver on any kind of track in any kind of car."

3. From the statements below, choose those that you believe the author would agree with.

☐ a. Mario Andretti was an especially skilled driver.

☐ b. Andretti remained a reckless driver throughout his career.

☐ c. Many drivers have matched or exceeded Andretti in skill.

4. Choose the statement below that is the weakest argument for taking up auto racing.

☐ a. Racing is a relatively safe sport.

☐ b. Racing is exciting.

☐ c. In racing, you can test your own personal limits.

_______ Number of correct answers

Record your personal assessment of your work on the Critical Thinking Chart on page 136.

Summarizing and Paraphrasing

Follow the directions provided for question 1. Put an X in the box next to the correct answer for question 2.

1. Look for the important ideas and events in paragraphs 3 and 4. Summarize those paragraphs in one or two sentences.

____

____

____

2. Choose the sentence that correctly restates the following sentence from the article:

   "Although Mario won only one race, he had enough second and third place finishes to win [the title]."

☐ a. Mario won two or three races, but came in second in one race.

☐ b. Mario won the title by finishing second or third in several races and by winning one race.

☐ c. Since Mario did not win more than one race, it is strange that he was given the title.

_______ Number of correct answers

Record your personal assessment of your work on the Critical Thinking Chart on page 136.

Critical Thinking

Put an X in the box next to the correct answer for questions 1, 3, and 4. Follow the directions provided for questions 2 and 5.

1. From what the article told about Mario's father, you can conclude that he

☐ a. was unreasonable and overly strict with his children.

☐ b. loved his children and cared about their safety.

☐ c. didn't care at all about his children's wishes.

2. Choose from the letters below to correctly complete the following statement. Write the letters on the lines.

   In the article, _______ and _______ are alike in their love of auto racing.

   a. Mario Andretti

   b. Aldo Andretti

   c. Mario and Aldo's father

3. What was the effect of the injuries and deaths of the participants in the driving program in Italy?

☐ a. Aldo decided that auto racing was too dangerous for him.

☐ b. The Andretti family moved to the United States.

☐ c. The program was soon canceled.

4. How is Mario Andretti an example of a daredevil?

☐ a. Mario gladly took part in a dangerous sport.

☐ b. Mario was a skillful driver.

☐ c. Mario won several awards in different categories.

5. In which paragraph did you find your information or details to answer question 3?

____

_______ Number of correct answers

Record your personal assessment of your work on the Critical Thinking Chart on page 136.

Personal Response

I agree with the author because

____

____

____

____

Self-Assessment

While reading the article, I found it easiest to

____

____

____

____

JULIE KRONE
Jockey

Horses frequently bunch up as they come out of the gate at the start of a race. Julie Krone kept her horse outside of this kind of traffic the day she was thrown from her mount at Saratoga.

Every August the best horses and jockeys gather at the Saratoga Race Course in Saratoga Springs, New York. In 1993, Julie Krone was there. She was one of the world's best jockeys—male or female. Krone was having an excellent Saratoga meet. One day she rode home five winners. Only two jockeys in history had ever done that at Saratoga.

2 It was August 30th, the last day of the meet. Krone had already started packing and getting ready to leave town. She had only two mounts that day—in the third and seventh races. In the third race she was scheduled to ride a big filly named Seattle Way. For a pro like Julie Krone, it seemed like just another race. But while it would start out routinely, it wouldn't end that way.

3 The horses broke from the starting gate smoothly. Krone kept Seattle Way on the outside and out of traffic, slowly urging the horse to give her more speed. Krone had Seattle Way in perfect position as the field rounded the far turn. Then, without warning, the horse on her inside veered

out and bumped into Seattle Way. "I don't remember falling," Krone said later. But as the crowd gasped she went flying.

4 Krone was fortunate she wasn't killed. She landed on her ankle and then tumbled head over heels. Out of the corner of her eye, she spotted Two Is Trouble thundering straight at her. The 1,200-pound horse trampled right over Krone, stepping on her chest. Luckily, she was wearing a flak jacket; otherwise the blow might have been fatal. After the racehorse ran over her, "there was nothing," Krone said. "No horses, no thunder, no whirlwind of color. Just the dry turf under my back...and pain."

5 The ambulance arrived within a few seconds. Paramedics rushed Krone to the hospital. Her ankle was a real mess. She needed two operations to put it back together. Doctors had to insert two plates and 14 screws in her ankle. Krone would not ride in another race for nearly nine months.

6 At the time of her accident, Julie Krone was riding on top of the world. In 1989, she had been on the cover of *Sports Illustrated*. In 1991, she had become the first female jockey to ride in the Belmont Stakes, part of racing's famous Triple Crown. And in the spring of 1993, she had won the Belmont Stakes aboard Colonial Affair. She was looking forward to riding her 3,000th winner. Only 61 jockeys in American history had won that many races.

7 Krone had worked hard for her success. Her line of work was fraught with danger. Horse racing is the only sport where an ambulance follows right behind the competitors. It's one of the few sports where people check to see how many competitors finish the race. That's because once in a while, someone—such as Julie Krone on that awful August day—doesn't reach the finish line.

8 If being a jockey is hard, then being a female jockey is even harder. Today, men and women compete on equal terms. That is, female jockeys compete directly against men. But until 1968, state racing commissions refused to allow women to ride at all. In 1970, jockey Diane Crump broke new ground by being the first female to ride in the Kentucky Derby. Soon other women also began to ride. Most, however, rode at minor tracks. They did not compete at the major tracks against the best in the sport. Many trainers felt that women, with their gentle touch, were adequate for working with younger horses. But these same trainers did not believe women were strong enough to handle older, stronger horses.

9 Julie Krone began her career during these transitional years. She had learned to ride even before she could walk. She rode horses around her family's farm in Michigan. Often she jumped fences and rode standing up in the saddle. At the age of five, she won a ribbon at a county fair

Jockey Julie Krone hasn't given up racing horses in spite of the serious injuries she has suffered.

horse show competing in the 21-and-under age division. But little Julie had bigger dreams than winning ribbons at county fairs. She wanted to race. "I was always going to be a jockey, and a great one, too," she recalled.

10 By the age of 16, Krone had left high school and had begun her life as a jockey. Many trainers wanted nothing to do with a girl 4'10½" tall and weighing barely 100 pounds. But some were willing to give her a chance. Slowly, Krone proved just how good she could be. In 1982, she won 155 races at Atlantic City. Her record was exceptional enough to earn her the riding title at that track, making her the first woman ever to win such a title at a major track.

11 She won the title again in 1983. Then she began to move up the ladder, riding at bigger and bigger tracks. At last, in 1987, she moved to Aqueduct in New York City, where she faced the top jockeys in the sport. On opening day, Krone rode four winners. It was clear that she could handle the best. One reporter wrote, "She is an athlete who must be compared not to other female riders, but in the context of her performance against men."

12 By then, Krone was well on her way to earning her nickname as "the Band-Aid Kid." In 1983, she fell during a race and broke her back. It took her four months to recuperate. In 1989, she fell again, this time breaking her left wrist. Her doctors had to insert a plate and 14 screws. Krone lost eight months of racing. Then in 1993 came the near-fatal spill at Saratoga.

13 Despite the pain and the danger, Julie Krone didn't stop racing. After the Saratoga accident, she spent more than eight months recovering. Then, while still needing crutches to walk, she climbed back into the saddle. "What racing teaches you is to go forward, 365 days, until you fall off," she explained. "You never have time to look back."

14 In 1995, Krone fell once again. This time she fractured her left wrist. She lost two more months, but then—as before—returned to racing. At the time of her return, she had already won several million dollars and thousands of races. When asked why she didn't just retire, she explained that something inside kept her going back to the track despite the injuries. Something kept her fighting for victories. And what was that something? "That something," she said, is "simply me."

If you have been timed while reading this article, enter your reading time below. Then turn to the Words-per-Minute Table on page 133 and look up your reading speed (words per minute). Enter your reading speed on the graph on page 134.

Reading Time: Lesson 11

_________ : _________

Minutes *Seconds*

A Finding the Main Idea

One statement below expresses the main idea of the article. One statement is too general, or too broad. The other statement explains only part of the article; it is too narrow. Label the statements using the following key:

M—Main Idea **B—Too Broad** **N—Too Narrow**

_______ 1. Horse racing is a sport that has traditionally been dominated by men.

_______ 2. In 1987, jockey Julie Krone won 155 races at Atlantic City, earning herself the riding title at that track.

_______ 3. Julie Krone is an exceptionally skillful jockey who continues to compete and win horse races in spite of danger and injuries.

_______ Score 15 points for a correct M answer.

_______ Score 5 points for each correct B or N answer.

_______ **Total Score:** Finding the Main Idea

B Recalling Facts

How well do you remember the facts in the article? Put an X in the box next to the answer that correctly completes each statement about the article.

1. In 1989, Julie Krone appeared on the cover of

☐ a. *Sports Illustrated.*
☐ b. *People.*
☐ c. *Life.*

2. Krone was the first woman to compete in the

☐ a. Kentucky Derby.
☐ b. Belmont Stakes.
☐ c. Preakness.

3. Krone grew up on her family's farm in

☐ a. Michigan.
☐ b. Kentucky.
☐ c. New York.

4. Krone was known as the "Band-Aid Kid" because

☐ a. the company that makes Band-Aids sponsored her.
☐ b. she rode a horse called Band-Aid.
☐ c. she got injured frequently.

5. Aqueduct in New York City is considered to be a

☐ a. major racetrack.
☐ b. minor racetrack.
☐ c. woman's racetrack.

Score 5 points for each correct answer.

_______ **Total Score:** Recalling Facts

C Making Inferences

When you combine your own experience and information from a text to draw a conclusion that is not directly stated in that text, you are making an inference. Below are five statements that may or may not be inferences based on information in the article. Label the statements using the following key:

C—Correct Inference **F—Faulty Inference**

_______ 1. The men that Krone competed against treated her more gently because she was a woman.

_______ 2. Krone heals more slowly than most people do.

_______ 3. Krone is a brave competitor.

_______ 4. People who knew Krone as a child could have predicted that she would one day become a professional jockey.

_______ 5. It takes more strength to handle a mature horse than it does to handle a young horse.

Score 5 points for each correct answer.

_______ **Total Score:** Making Inferences

D Using Words Precisely

Each numbered sentence below contains an underlined word or phrase from the article. Following the sentence are three definitions. One definition is closest to the meaning of the underlined word. One definition is opposite or nearly opposite. Label those two definitions using the following key. Do not label the remaining definition.

C—Closest **O—Opposite or Nearly Opposite**

1. Then, without warning, the horse on her inside veered out and bumped into Seattle Way.

_______ a. kicked

_______ b. continued on a planned path

_______ c. changed direction

2. Her line of work was fraught with danger.

_______ a. filled with

_______ b. prohibited because of

_______ c. empty of

3. Many trainers felt that women, with their gentle touch, were adequate for working with younger horses.

_______ a. famous

_______ b. unacceptable

_______ c. all right

4. Julie Krone began her career during these transitional years.

_______ a. unchanging

_______ b. passing from one stage to the next

_______ c. historic

5. Her record was exceptional enough to earn her the riding title at that track, making her the first woman ever to win such a title at a major track.

_______ a. average

_______ b. bold

_______ c. superior

_______ Score 3 points for each correct C answer.

_______ Score 2 points for each correct O answer.

_______ **Total Score:** Using Words Precisely

Enter the four total scores in the spaces below, and add them together to find your Reading Comprehension Score. Then record your score on the graph on page 135.

Score	Question Type	Lesson 11
_______	Finding the Main Idea	
_______	Recalling Facts	
_______	Making Inferences	
_______	Using Words Precisely	
_______	**Reading Comprehension Score**	

Author's Approach

Put an X in the box next to the correct answer.

1. The author uses the first paragraph of the article to

☐ a. inform the reader about the general topic the article will explore.

☐ b. describe the qualities of professional horse racers.

☐ c. compare Saratoga Race Course and other racetracks.

2. What is the author's purpose in writing "Julie Krone: Jockey"?

☐ a. To encourage the reader to become a professional athlete

☐ b. To describe a situation in which a woman proved she could do a particular job as well as a man

☐ c. To emphasize the similarities between horseracing and auto racing

3. In this article, the statement "Krone kept Seattle Way on the outside and out of traffic" means

☐ a. Krone kept her horse away from cars near the racetrack.

☐ b. Krone kept her horse away from other horses in the race.

☐ c. Krone was afraid to take the lead.

4. How is the author's purpose for writing the article expressed in paragraph 14?

☐ a. The paragraph says that Krone fractured her wrist in 1995.

☐ b. The paragraph points out that Krone won millions of dollars.

☐ c. The paragraph points out that Krone wanted to compete despite the threat of injuries.

_______ Number of correct answers

Record your personal assessment of your work on the Critical Thinking Chart on page 136.

Summarizing and Paraphrasing

Follow the directions provided for questions 1 and 2. Put an X in the box next to the correct answer for question 3.

1. Complete the following one-sentence summary of the article using the lettered phrases from the phrase bank below. Write the letters on the lines.

Phrase Bank:

a. why it was unusual for a woman to be competing in a major horse race

b. Krone's explanation of why she keeps riding

c. a description of a race at Saratoga in which Krone was badly injured

The article about "Julie Krone: Jockey" begins with ________, goes on to explain ________, and ends with ________.

2. Reread paragraph 9 in the article. Below, write a summary of the paragraph in no more than 25 words.

____

____

____

____

Reread your summary and decide whether it covers the important ideas in the paragraph. Next, decide how to shorten the summary to 15 words or less without leaving out any essential information. Write this summary below.

____

____

3. Read the statement about the article below. Then read the paraphrase of that statement. Choose the reason that best tells why the paraphrase does not say the same thing as the statement.

Statement: The 1,200-pound horse stepped on Krone's chest, but she survived because she was wearing a flak jacket.

Paraphrase: It was just luck that Krone survived the accident in which she was trampled by a 1,200-pound horse.

☐ a. Paraphrase says too much.

☐ b. Paraphrase doesn't say enough.

☐ c. Paraphrase doesn't agree with the statement about the article.

________ Number of correct answers

Record your personal assessment of your work on the Critical Thinking Chart on page 136.

Critical Thinking

Put an X in the box next to the correct answer for questions 1, 2, and 4. Follow the directions provided for question 3.

1. Which of the following statements from the article is an opinion rather than a fact?

☐ a. "But these same trainers did not believe women were strong enough to handle older, stronger horses."

☐ b. "In 1983, she fell during a race and broke her back."

☐ c. "If being a jockey is hard, then being a female jockey is even harder."

CRITICAL THINKING

2. From what Julie Krone said, you can predict that she will

☐ a. probably die in an accident on the racetrack.

☐ b. continue to ride as long as she is physically able to do so.

☐ c. give up racing as soon as possible.

3. Read paragraph 3. Then choose from the letters below to correctly complete the following statement. Write the letters on the lines.

According to paragraph 3,__________ because __________.

a. Krone fell from her horse

b. Seattle Way was in perfect position to win the race

c. another horse bumped into her horse

4. If you were a jockey, how could you use the information in the article to win races?

☐ a. Like Krone, get your picture on the cover of a magazine.

☐ b. Like Krone, suffer many serious injuries.

☐ c. Like Krone, understand that you have to keep trying.

_________ Number of correct answers

Record your personal assessment of your work on the Critical Thinking Chart on page 136.

Personal Response

I know the feeling

____

____

____

____

Self-Assessment

I can't really understand how

____

____

____

____

CLIMBING FROZEN WATERFALLS

The man's cry echoed through the frozen White Mountains of New Hampshire. His two safety screws should have saved him, but they both failed. The man fell 45 feet down Cannon Cliff and crashed onto the ground, breaking two bones in his right leg as well as a bone in his left shoulder. His two climbing partners scrambled to his aid. They put a splint on his leg and tied his helmet to his foot so they could more easily drag his broken leg through the snow. Even so, it took them four hours to get to the nearest road.

2 Welcome to the world of ice climbing. The sport began in the late 1960s and has been growing in popularity ever since. The idea is simple. You trudge deep into the mountains in the dead of winter looking for a huge frozen waterfall. These waterfalls are hundreds of feet high. Some are attached to the walls of sheer cliffs. Others hang like giant icicles, not attached to anything except at their top and base. Either way, because water falls straight down, the climb is straight up.

3 Ice climbing isn't for timid souls. The names of the climbs alone would frighten

Ice-climber Rick Wyatt climbs a frozen waterfall in Provo Canyon, Utah.

away most sensible people. Who, for example, would want to climb Casket Quarry in Minnesota? How about Wicked Wanda and the Weeping Wall in the Canadian Rockies? New York's Gorillas in the Mist doesn't sound too user-friendly. Neither does The Fang in Colorado.

4 Most people don't want any part of climbing these frozen marvels. Their motto is "look, don't climb." There is, however, a growing pack of daredevils who roam the world looking for ice to climb. For them, the ice is a challenge. "You've got to look right into the bottom of yourself," says Rick Wyatt. "It's the place where all the bull stops. Either you can do it or you can't."

5 Anyone who chooses to ice climb must have the proper equipment. Each climber needs two special eight-inch curved axes with serrated teeth. A climber uses one in each hand, plunging the axes deep into the ice as he or she moves upward. Another vital piece of equipment is crampons, sharp pointed metal cleats that attach to boots. Two of the prongs on the crampons slant forward and can be kicked into the ice. Counting both arms and legs, a climber has four points of contact with the ice. To stay secure on a vertical wall of ice, three points should be attached to the ice at any one time. That makes ice climbing a slow chop-chop, step-step process.

6 One other piece of equipment is essential for safety. Climbers put ice screws into the ice to protect themselves if they fall. One end of a rope is attached to the screw, the other end to the climber. If a climber falls, the rope will stop him or her—provided the ice screw holds. Sometimes screws are not properly set or the ice is weak, in which case the screw will pull out of the ice and the climber will continue to plunge downward.

7 The best scenario, of course, is to avoid falling. As climber Bill Erler puts it, "Falling is not recommended for ice climbers." There are plenty of good reasons for that. For openers, a fall could kill you. It happens every year. Climbers might not realize that the sun has weakened the ice in the middle of a long climb. Suddenly, halfway up the icicle, the ice gives way and the climber tumbles to his or her death. Occasionally an avalanche will sweep a climber away. High winds, sudden storms, a broken prong, and a dropped ax are all hazards that can lead to deadly falls. "If you do [ice climbing] hard for 15 years," says John Bouchard, "you've got a 50% chance of dying...maybe 30%."

Marc Twight climbs the famous Weeping Wall in the Canadian Rockies in Banff, Canada.

[8] A fall that doesn't kill can still hurt. Broken ribs and bones are commonplace whenever a climber falls. During a fall, a climber might catch a prong on the ice, causing his ankle to snap like a twig. Another hazard of falling is getting stabbed by your own ax. Then, too, there are all the internal injuries that can result when you slam into an unforgiving pile of rocks or wall of ice. Climber Alex Lowe broke a prong and fell 170 feet before his safety rope slammed him into a wall. The blow knocked Lowe unconscious. He was lucky to come out of the day alive.

[9] Ice climbing holds other dangers, as well. Among these are frostbite, exhaustion, and hypothermia. Brittle ice is also bad news for a climber. The blow of an ax can shatter such ice into many flat fragments—called "dinner plates"—which rain down on the climber. Such a piece once fell into Lowe's eye, slicing his cornea.

[10] On top of the dangers, ice climbing holds certain inconveniences. Finding a good place to climb isn't always easy. Frozen waterfalls are often far off the beaten path. Says Mike O'Donnell, "I've sometimes walked a zillion miles...in search of 90 feet of frozen water."

[11] Some places have great ice one year and none the next. Ice is fickle, changing not only from year to year, but from day to day and even from hour to hour. It has been said that you can never swim in the same river twice because the water is always changing. Well, a similar saying holds true for ice climbing. You can never make the same climb twice.

[12] Still, climbers have been searching for a place where they can be fairly certain to find solid ice to climb no matter when they reach it. In Ouray, Colorado, they have found such a place. The world's first ice-climbing park was built there in 1995. It has its own water pipes and sprinklers. The park has more than 45 routes to the top of the 120-foot climb. A novice thinking of giving the sport a try should probably avoid the routes named "Bloody Sunday" and "Root Canal."

[13] Clearly, ice climbing isn't for everyone. But to those who are attracted to it, it's almost like a religion. Being so close to death tends to focus the mind like prayer. Climbers often talk about being in a Zen-like state of consciousness. And the thrill never grows old. "It's a mystical experience," says Antoine Savelli. "The actual act of climbing is so immediate...addicting. It never fades."

If you have been timed while reading this article, enter your reading time below. Then turn to the Words-per-Minute Table on page 133 and look up your reading speed (words per minute). Enter your reading speed on the graph on page 134.

Reading Time: Lesson 12

_______ : _______

Minutes *Seconds*

A Finding the Main Idea

One statement below expresses the main idea of the article. One statement is too general, or too broad. The other statement explains only part of the article; it is too narrow. Label the statements using the following key:

M—Main Idea **B—Too Broad** **N—Too Narrow**

_______ 1. A relatively new winter sport is now becoming popular with daredevils.

_______ 2. One of the biggest dangers in the sport of ice climbing is falling; falls can lead to injury or even death.

_______ 3. The sport of ice climbing—climbing frozen waterfalls—is becoming popular with people who crave danger in their pastimes.

_______ Score 15 points for a correct M answer.

_______ Score 5 points for each correct B or N answer.

_______ **Total Score:** Finding the Main Idea

Recalling Facts

How well do you remember the facts in the article? Put an X in the box next to the answer that correctly completes each statement about the article.

1. The sport of ice climbing is said to have begun in the
- ☐ a. 19th century.
- ☐ b. 1960s.
- ☐ c. 1990s.

2. Crampons are
- ☐ a. sharp metal cleats that attach to boots.
- ☐ b. strong ropes.
- ☐ c. long screws that climbers insert into the ice.

3. Climbers tie ropes first to themselves and then to
- ☐ a. their buddies.
- ☐ b. screws they put in the ice.
- ☐ c. their axes.

4. In ice climbing, dangerous ice fragments are sometimes called
- ☐ a. ice cream cones.
- ☐ b. dinner plates.
- ☐ c. mirrors.

5. In 1995, an ice-climbing park was built in
- ☐ a. Los Angeles, California.
- ☐ b. Rocky Mountain National Park.
- ☐ c. Ouray, Colorado.

Score 5 points for each correct answer.

_______ **Total Score:** Recalling Facts

C Making Inferences

When you combine your own experience and information from a text to draw a conclusion that is not directly stated in that text, you are making an inference. Below are five statements that may or may not be inferences based on information in the article. Label the statements using the following key:

C—Correct Inference **F—Faulty Inference**

_______ 1. If you are just giving ice climbing a try, you probably don't need to use all the protective equipment that regular ice climbers use.

_______ 2. Ice climbers must be willing to risk getting badly hurt.

_______ 3. The best time to go ice climbing is on a warm, sunny day.

_______ 4. Having a safety rope tied around an ice climber prevents him or her from being hurt at all in a fall.

_______ 5. It is a good idea never to go ice climbing alone.

Score 5 points for each correct answer.

_______ **Total Score:** Making Inferences

D Using Words Precisely

Each numbered sentence below contains an underlined word or phrase from the article. Following the sentence are three definitions. One definition is closest to the meaning of the underlined word. One definition is opposite or nearly opposite. Label those two definitions using the following key. Do not label the remaining definition.

C—Closest **O—Opposite or Nearly Opposite**

1. You trudge deep into the mountains in the dead of winter looking for a huge frozen waterfall.

_______ a. skip

_______ b. look

_______ c. walk slowly and heavily

2. Each climber needs two special eight-inch curved axes with serrated teeth.

_______ a. jagged

_______ b. smooth

_______ c. tiny

3. Broken ribs and bones are commonplace whenever a climber falls.

_______ a. unusual

_______ b. tragic

_______ c. ordinary

4. A novice thinking of giving the sport a try should probably avoid the routes named "Bloody Sunday" and "Root Canal."

_______ a. careless person

_______ b. beginner

_______ c. experienced participant

5. "It's a mystical experience," says Antoine Savelli.

_______ a. spiritual

_______ b. practical and earthbound

_______ c. funny

_______ Score 3 points for each correct C answer.

_______ Score 2 points for each correct O answer.

_______ **Total Score:** Using Words Precisely

Enter the four total scores in the spaces below, and add them together to find your Reading Comprehension Score. Then record your score on the graph on page 135.

Score	Question Type	Lesson 12
_______	Finding the Main Idea	
_______	Recalling Facts	
_______	Making Inferences	
_______	Using Words Precisely	
_______	**Reading Comprehension Score**	

Author's Approach

Put an X in the box next to the correct answer.

1. The main purpose of the first paragraph is to

☐ a. compare ice climbing and mountain climbing.

☐ b. describe some of the risks involved in ice climbing.

☐ c. create a light-hearted mood.

2. What does the author imply by saying "There is, however, a growing pack of daredevils who roam the world looking for ice to climb"?

☐ a. To find good ice you always need to travel long distances.

☐ b. Ice climbers enjoy traveling as much as ice climbing.

☐ c. The perfect icicle for climbing can be difficult to find.

3. The author tells this story mainly by

☐ a. telling different stories about the same topic.

☐ b. telling one person's experiences with ice climbing.

☐ c. using his or her imagination and creativity.

_______ Number of correct answers

Record your personal assessment of your work on the Critical Thinking Chart on page 136.

Summarizing and Paraphrasing

Follow the directions provided for question 1. Put an X in the box next to the correct answer for the other questions.

1. Look for the important ideas and events in paragraphs 10 and 11. Summarize those paragraphs in one or two sentences.

____

____

____

2. Below are summaries of the article. Choose the summary that says all the most important things about the article but in the fewest words.

☐ a. Even though ice climbers are careful, they still run the risk of hurting themselves badly.

☐ b. Ice climbers are aware that they run the risk of being hurt or even killed in falls, and that is why they equip themselves with gear that helps them grip the side of the waterfall securely.

☐ c. Ice climbers not only accept, but also welcome, the risks that are part of their sport of climbing frozen waterfalls.

3. Read the statement about the article below. Then read the paraphrase of that statement. Choose the reason that best tells why the paraphrase does not say the same thing as the statement.

Statement: Even though the prongs on crampons are necessary for staying secure on a wall of ice, they can hurt climbers if they catch on the ice during a fall.

Paraphrase: If you fall off a frozen waterfall, the prongs on your crampons may catch on ice on the way down.

☐ a. Paraphrase says too much.

☐ b. Paraphrase doesn't say enough.

☐ c. Paraphrase doesn't agree with the statement about the article.

_______ Number of correct answers

Record your personal assessment of your work on the Critical Thinking Chart on page 136.

Critical Thinking

Follow the directions provided for questions 1, 2, and 4. Put an X in the box next to the correct answer for question 3.

1. For each statement below, write O if it expresses an opinion or write F if it expresses a fact.

_______ a. Some of the waterfalls that ice climbers tackle are hundreds of feet high.

_______ b. Ice climbers are the most daring of all winter sports enthusiasts.

_______ c. If the ice is weak, the screws that climbers insert in the waterfall can pull out.

2. Choose from the letters below to correctly complete the following statement. Write the letters on the lines.

   On the positive side, ________, but on the negative side ________.

   a. ice climbing is dangerous
   b. ice climbing is exciting and fun
   c. ice climbers use small axes to dig into the ice

3. What was the cause of the injury to Alex Lowe's cornea?

☐ a. A sharp piece of ice fell into his eye.
☐ b. He fell into a jagged rock.
☐ c. He hit his eye with his small axe.

4. In which paragraph did you find your information or details to answer question 3?

____

________ Number of correct answers

Record your personal assessment of your work on the Critical Thinking Chart on page 136.

Personal Response

What was most surprising or interesting to you about this article?

____

____

____

____

Self-Assessment

Which concepts or ideas from the article were difficult to understand?

____

____

____

____

Which were easy to understand?

____

____

____

____

HOLLYWOOD STUNTWOMEN

When most people fill out their résumés, they list such ordinary items as what schools they attended and where they have worked. Maybe they will include the names of a few people who know them well. A Hollywood stuntwoman's résumé, however, isn't like a normal résumé. For one thing, photos are essential. So, too, are descriptions of physical traits such as height, weight, and hair color. After all, if the stuntwoman is going to "double" for a movie star, there has to be a certain physical resemblance.

2 Still, the right look alone won't get a stuntwoman a job. Movie directors want to know what special risk-taking abilities she has. So stuntwomen will list on their résumés such skills as "high speed chases," "fight scenes," "stair falls," "kick boxing," "full burns," and "motorcycle flips." These skills are important. After all, when the script calls for the star to fall off a high building or to ski down a glacier or drive a car at tremendous speeds, who's going to do it? Nine times out of ten, it won't be the big-name star. It will be a stuntwoman whose name no one in the audience knows.

Hollywood stunt person Sonia Davis leaps from one building to another while filming a movie.

[3] Imagine this typical Hollywood scene. The cameras are rolling at Pier 66 in Fort Lauderdale, Florida. Actress Cindy Crawford is caught in her apartment building when a huge bomb goes off. The blast blows poor Cindy through her sliding glass door. With shards of broken glass raining down on her head, Cindy bounces off the balcony and then plunges head over heels into the harbor far below. Spectators gasp with delight as Cindy swims safely to the shore. Of course, it's not really Cindy Crawford who's out there risking her life. It's Anita Hart—Cindy's stunt double. Such scenes are staples for most Hollywood action movies.

[4] How risky are these spectacular stunts? They certainly look dangerous on the screen, and most stars don't want any part in them. But being a stuntwomen is a profession, and the people who have chosen this profession don't think of themselves as foolhardy. "Stunt performers are not daredevils," insists Jadie David, one of Hollywood's first African-American stuntwomen. "They do a job and calculate the risk and minimize it. They are not thrill seekers. You're being paid for your skill."

[5] Other Hollywood stuntwomen have said pretty much the same thing. They all maintain that if you know what you are doing, the job of performing stunts is not dangerous. They talk about the emphasis on safety and modern equipment. And they argue that life itself is risky and that you could get killed crossing the street.

[6] Stuntwomen do admit, however, that they work with a very small margin of error. If you jump out of an airplane and the parachute opens the way it should, it's no big deal. But if the parachute doesn't open, well...stuntwomen know the risks are real. LaFaye Baker, a veteran stuntwoman says, "You can't take anything for granted. The smallest thing could cost you an accident." When something does go awry, the results are often tragic. "Four of my good friends," says Diane Peterson, "have been killed in this kind of work."

[7] Accidents can also result in crippling injuries. Heidi von Beltz had the world at her fingertips. As a teenager she was a superior athlete, excelling in tennis, skiing, and horseback riding. Von Beltz was pretty enough to find work as a model. And since she loved to take on new physical challenges, she eventually became a Hollywood stuntwoman. What happened to Heidi von Beltz shows how truly hazardous this kind of work can be.

[8] In 1980, the 24-year-old von Beltz was working in a film called *The Cannonball Run* with Burt Reynolds. Hal Needham, a former stuntman, directed the movie. One key scene called for von Beltz, who was doubling for Farrah Fawcett, to be a passenger in a speeding car weaving

Skydiving can be a risky stunt if the parachute doesn't operate correctly. Here, stunt person Kay Kimmel leaps from a plane.

through traffic. "We did it once," recalled von Beltz, "and it was fine."

9 But the director wanted to try it again at higher speeds. This time it wasn't fine. The driver tried desperately to control the car, but the vehicle didn't respond quickly enough and the car slammed into a van. Von Beltz, who hadn't thought the stunt was particularly dangerous, hadn't put on her seat belt. The force of the crash drove her into the dashboard and windshield, fracturing her spinal cord and smashing several neck vertebrae. "When [film crew workers] ran up to the car," she recalled, "they found my head literally hanging down on my back. That's how disconnected it was—it was hanging by a thread. My neck had exploded—part of it was missing."

10 Heidi von Beltz survived, but she was paralyzed from the neck down. Her doctors gave her five years to live. They suggested that her parents put her in an institution. However, her parents rejected that advice and took their daughter home. Von Beltz did not die as her doctors had predicted. Instead, after years and years of therapy, she made a remarkable recovery, learning to sit up and stand by herself.

11 The accident had a few silver linings. The movie industry passed new rules regarding stunt safety, so that today everyone in a stunt car is required to wear a seat belt. Also, all directors are prohibited from changing stunts on location.

12 And, in a strange way, the crash helped Heidi von Beltz. She discovered that she didn't have to be a daredevil to enjoy life. "I was always so active that I would never have sat down long enough to learn what I've learned," she said. "I can't imagine going through this life and not knowing what I know now. I just had to break my neck to do it."

If you have been timed while reading this article, enter your reading time below. Then turn to the Words-per-Minute Table on page 133 and look up your reading speed (words per minute). Enter your reading speed on the graph on page 134.

Reading Time: Lesson 13

_______ : _______

Minutes *Seconds*

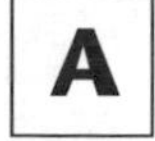

Finding the Main Idea

One statement below expresses the main idea of the article. One statement is too general, or too broad. The other statement explains only part of the article; it is too narrow. Label the statements using the following key:

M—Main Idea **B—Too Broad** **N—Too Narrow**

_______ 1. Hollywood stuntwomen fill in for actresses when the script calls for a dangerous stunt; their job takes superior physical abilities and a willingness to take risks.

_______ 2. One stuntwoman, Heidi von Beltz, had a terrible auto accident while she was filling in as actress Farrah Fawcett's double.

_______ 3. Stuntwomen are willing to take risks to make an exciting movie.

_______ Score 15 points for a correct M answer.

_______ Score 5 points for each correct B or N answer.

_______ **Total Score:** Finding the Main Idea

Recalling Facts

How well do you remember the facts in the article? Put an X in the box next to the answer that correctly completes each statement about the article.

1. A stuntwoman's résumé should include information about
- ☐ a. her height and weight.
- ☐ b. her religion.
- ☐ c. whether or not she has any children.

2. A stunt double must
- ☐ a. be able to drive a car and swim.
- ☐ b. be at least 21 years old.
- ☐ c. look like the person he or she is filling in for.

3. Stuntwoman Heidi von Beltz was injured when she
- ☐ a. crashed in a speeding car.
- ☐ b. fell from a tall building.
- ☐ c. jumped from an airplane.

4. As a result of the accident, von Beltz
- ☐ a. went blind.
- ☐ b. was paralyzed from the neck down.
- ☐ c. forgot her own name.

5. Now, movie directors may no longer
- ☐ a. use real people in dangerous stunts.
- ☐ b. film auto accidents.
- ☐ c. change any stunts on location.

Score 5 points for each correct answer.

_______ **Total Score:** Recalling Facts

C Making Inferences

When you combine your own experience and information from a text to draw a conclusion that is not directly stated in that text, you are making an inference. Below are five statements that may or may not be inferences based on information in the article. Label the statements using the following key:

C—Correct Inference **F—Faulty Inference**

_______ 1. Stuntwomen would rather act than perform dangerous stunts.

_______ 2. Because their job is so dangerous, stuntwomen are paid more than actresses.

_______ 3. Actresses are glad that there are stuntwomen to fill in for them in dangerous scenes.

_______ 4. Most stuntwomen are good athletes.

_______ 5. When you change a stunt on location, you run the risk of making it more dangerous than it should be.

Score 5 points for each correct answer.

_______ **Total Score:** Making Inferences

D Using Words Precisely

Each numbered sentence below contains an underlined word or phrase from the article. Following the sentence are three definitions. One definition is closest to the meaning of the underlined word. One definition is opposite or nearly opposite. Label those two definitions using the following key. Do not label the remaining definition.

C—Closest **O—Opposite or Nearly Opposite**

1. Such scenes are <u>staples</u> for most Hollywood action movies.

_______ a. basic elements

_______ b. unnecessary extras

_______ c. tools

2. They do a job and calculate the risk and <u>minimize</u> it.

_______ a. accept

_______ b. lessen

_______ c. make bigger

3. When something does go <u>awry</u>, the results are often tragic.

_______ a. right

_______ b. away

_______ c. wrong

4. As a teenager she was a superior athlete, <u>excelling</u> in tennis, skiing, and horseback riding.

_______ a. not doing as well as others

_______ b. showing extraordinary talent

_______ c. trying hard

5. One <u>key</u> scene called for von Beltz, who was doubling for Farrah Fawcett, to be a passenger in a speeding car weaving through traffic.

_______ a. important

_______ b. typical

_______ c. unnecessary

_______ Score 3 points for each correct C answer.

_______ Score 2 points for each correct O answer.

_______ **Total Score:** Using Words Precisely

Enter the four total scores in the spaces below, and add them together to find your Reading Comprehension Score. Then record your score on the graph on page 135.

Score	Question Type	Lesson 13
_______	Finding the Main Idea	
_______	Recalling Facts	
_______	Making Inferences	
_______	Using Words Precisely	
_______	**Reading Comprehension Score**	

Author's Approach

Put an X in the box next to the correct answer.

1. What is the author's purpose in writing "Hollywood Stuntwomen"?

☐ a. To encourage the reader to become a stunt double

☐ b. To inform the reader about the risks and rewards of being a stunt person

☐ c. To emphasize the similarities between a normal résumé and the résumé of a stuntwoman

2. From the statements below, choose those that you believe the author would agree with.

☐ a. Stuntwomen prepare themselves as well as they can for the stunts they are asked to do.

☐ b. Stuntwomen accept the fact that their jobs often involve danger.

☐ c. People who take up stunt work don't understand the risks they face; if they did, they would give up their jobs.

3. In this article, "Heidi von Beltz had the world at her fingertips" means

☐ a. Life was going well for Heidi von Beltz in many ways.

☐ b. Heidi von Beltz loved to travel.

☐ c. Heidi von Beltz was both a model and a stuntwoman.

_______ Number of correct answers

Record your personal assessment of your work on the Critical Thinking Chart on page 136.

Summarizing and Paraphrasing

Follow the directions provided for question 1. Put an X in the box next to the correct answer for question 2.

1. Look for the important ideas and events in paragraphs 4 and 5. Summarize those paragraphs in one or two sentences.

____

____

____

2. Choose the sentence that correctly restates the following sentence from the article:

   "But being a stuntwomen is a profession, and the people who have chosen this profession don't think of themselves as foolhardy."

   ☐ a. Professional people never take unnecessary chances.

   ☐ b. Stuntwomen believe that, as professionals, they know enough not to take unnecessary risks.

   ☐ c. Stuntwomen perform stunts for a living and so they are less likely than other women to take foolish chances.

_______ Number of correct answers

Record your personal assessment of your work on the Critical Thinking Chart on page 136.

Critical Thinking

Follow the directions provided for questions 1, 3, and 4. Put an X in the box next to the correct answer for questions 2 and 5.

1. For each statement below, write O if it expresses an opinion or write F if it expresses a fact.

   _______ a. After therapy, Heidi von Beltz was able to sit up and stand by herself.

   _______ b. Simply walking across the street poses a certain amount of risk.

   _______ c. No one should be allowed to risk death just to create an exciting scene for a movie.

2. From what LaFaye Baker said in paragraph 6, you can predict that before she does any stunt, she

   ☐ a. prepares her own parachute.

   ☐ b. relaxes and hopes for the best.

   ☐ c. checks and double-checks her safety precautions.

3. Choose from the letters below to correctly complete the following statement. Write the letters on the lines.

   In the article, _______ and _______ are alike because both are famous actresses.

   a. Cindy Crawford

   b. Farrah Fawcett

   c. Diane Peterson

CRITICAL THINKING

4. Reread paragraph 11. Then choose from the letters below to correctly complete the following statement. Write the letters on the lines.

   According to paragraph 11, ________ happened because ________.

   a. Heidi von Beltz was injured so badly when she wasn't wearing a seat belt
   b. Heidi von Beltz made a remarkable recovery
   c. new rules that require people in stunt cars to wear seat belts were passed

5. If you were looking for a way to get into show business, how could you use the information in the article to become a stunt person?

- [ ] a. Tell directors that you will not do any dangerous stunts.
- [ ] b. Write your own scripts in which the stunts are not risky.
- [ ] c. Be careful, but also be ready to accept the risks that come with the job of stunt person.

________ Number of correct answers

Record your personal assessment of your work on the Critical Thinking Chart on page 136.

Personal Response

I can't believe

____

____

____

____

Self-Assessment

Before reading this article, I already knew

____

____

____

____

CRISTINA SANCHEZ
Bullfighter

Cristina Sanchez's dream was to do just what her father had done. Like him, she wanted to be a matador and fight fierce bulls to the cheers of adoring fans. But Antonio Sanchez didn't want his young daughter to be a bullfighter. The bullring, he told her, was far too dangerous and besides, it was no place for a girl. He did everything he could to dissuade her. Whenever Cristina asked if she could become a bullfighter, he answered, "It is impossible." He went on to paint "a black, black picture" of his own sport. He told her of the bulls that had mauled him as well as other matadors. Antonio, in fact, had been gored so many times he had earned the nickname "Scar."

2 But all her father's dire warnings didn't scare Cristina off. She would say to him, "But in all that darkness there must be a tiny point of light, and that's where I will be able to pass." In the end, Antonio finally gave up. He sent Cristina to the most famous bullfighting school, in Madrid, Spain. He knew it was a long shot that his daughter would succeed in her effort to become a matador. He knew, also, that she could get killed, but in the end he had to let her follow her dream.

Although her father tried to discourage her, Cristina Sanchez achieved her goal of becoming a bullfighter. Here she salutes the crowd at a bullfight.

3 In Spain, most men greeted the notion of a woman bullfighter with jeers and laughter. They believed a woman's place was in the kitchen, not in the bullring. The term *machismo,* or male pride, comes from Spain. These men, called *machistas,* did not take kindly to any woman who tried to invade their territory. They insulted Cristina and taunted her without mercy. Cristina, who had grown up in the culture of bullfighting, was not surprised by their hostility. It just doubled her drive and determination. "I want to make the *machistas* eat their words," she often said. "[They] motivate me to fight bulls with even more anger, with more desire to demonstrate that women, just as men, deserve an opportunity."

4 Cristina Sanchez wasn't the first female bullfighter in Spain. But the half dozen or so earlier ones had either been mere curiosities or very unlucky. They never won the respect of the *machistas.* There was, for example, Juanita Cruz. When she fought in the 1930's, she drew huge crowds. But her career was interrupted by the Spanish Civil War. After the war, a strict law was passed prohibiting female matadors. Cruz never fought again in Spain. Frustrated, she had all the photos and articles about her career burned just before her death in 1981.

5 In 1974, the Spanish Supreme Court overturned the law against female matadors. Its decision opened the door for Angela Hernandez. But Hernandez paid a high price for the opportunity. Bulls broke her arms, wrists, clavicle, fingers, and back. They gored her 17 times. One bull ripped out two vertebrae from her spine, reducing her height by nearly an inch. In 1989, one bull's horn dug into the back of her knee and came out the front. And, to top it off, she never won the respect of the

Cristina Sanchez has had to overcome deeply ingrained prejudice against female bullfighters.

machistas. Said one old bullfighter, "Angela? No skill, no presence...nothing."

6 Still, Cristina Sanchez willingly took on all the dangers and all the prejudice. She graduated first in her class at the bullfighting school in Madrid. Slowly, she worked her way up through the bush leagues of bullfighting. She began by fighting two-year-old bulls in small rinks. Then she moved on to three-year-old bulls in larger arenas. It wasn't easy. Even small bulls can be awfully dangerous. Three times they gored her seriously, twice in her right thigh and once in her stomach.

7 And then there were the ever-present loudmouths. Despite her supreme grace and showmanship, Cristina was still taunted by spectators. In the smaller rinks, their foul catcalls were hard to ignore. Somehow, though, she managed. After a good fight, one of the ears from the dead bull is often presented to the matador. Sometimes, Cristina would take the severed ear and scornfully hurl it at her tormentors.

8 At last, on May 25, 1996, Cristina Sanchez made it to the major leagues of bullfighting. She faced and defeated a fully-grown four-year-old bull. That made her a *matador de toros* at the age of 24. Even the most macho of Spanish men had to admit she was pretty good. Cristina quickly became a fan favorite, earning more than a million dollars a year.

9 But why does she put her life on the line this way? After all, matadors do get killed every once in a while and there are hundreds of gorings each year. "It's a feeling," she says. "Something that makes me feel whole, complete and satisfied with my life. No one and nothing can make me feel that way, that passion I feel when I'm with a bull." Cristina goes on to say that when she is in the bullring, the outcome of a fight doesn't really matter. "You don't care either way if the bull gets you or not because of the sheer pleasure."

10 Well, say some critics, she may not worry about dying in the ring, but what about the poor bull? Every year hundreds of protestors gather outside the larger bullrings to decry the brutality of bull-fighting. Over 10,000 bulls die each year in the ring. Does Cristina ever pity the bull? "Never," she answers. "If he is a good bull, combative and generous in his fight, I sometimes feel badly that we have to part ways. But all bulls, like all men, eventually die. It is more glorious to die in a ring than a slaughterhouse."

11 Cristina Sanchez has overcome both man and beast. Still, it could all come to a bloody end any time she steps in a bull-ring. She is at the top of her sport. That means she must fight the biggest and fiercest bulls. Cristina Sanchez has a fatalistic vision of what might happen someday. One day, just before entering the ring, she said, "You know that any minute now, [the bull] can get you, and you won't be able to do anything about it."

If you have been timed while reading this article, enter your reading time below. Then turn to the Words-per-Minute Table on page 133 and look up your reading speed (words per minute). Enter your reading speed on the graph on page 134.

Reading Time: Lesson 14

________ : ________

Minutes *Seconds*

A Finding the Main Idea

One statement below expresses the main idea of the article. One statement is too general, or too broad. The other statement explains only part of the article; it is too narrow. Label the statements using the following key:

M—Main Idea **B—Too Broad** **N—Too Narrow**

_____ 1. Bullfighter Cristina Sanchez sometimes throws the bull's ear at her hecklers in the crowd, showing her scorn for them.

_____ 2. Bullfighting is a dangerous sport that is popular in Spain.

_____ 3. Cristina Sanchez is succeeding in a sport that has traditionally been reserved for men only—bullfighting.

_____ Score 15 points for a correct M answer.

_____ Score 5 points for each correct B or N answer.

_____ **Total Score:** Finding the Main Idea

B Recalling Facts

How well do you remember the facts in the article? Put an X in the box next to the answer that correctly completes each statement about the article.

1. Cristina Sanchez's father was a
   - ☐ a. teacher.
   - ☐ b. bullfighter.
   - ☐ c. painter.
2. Early in her career, when Sanchez fought, men in the crowd
   - ☐ a. insulted and taunted her.
   - ☐ b. cheered for her.
   - ☐ c. threw tomatoes at her.
3. Bullfighter Juanita Cruz's career was cut short by
   - ☐ a. World War I.
   - ☐ b. World War II.
   - ☐ c. the Spanish Civil War.
4. At the end of a good bullfight, the matador is presented with
   - ☐ a. the bull's ear.
   - ☐ b. a medal.
   - ☐ c. a gold cup.
5. Protesters estimate that about
   - ☐ a. 1,000 bulls are killed in the ring every year.
   - ☐ b. 10,000 bulls are killed in the ring every year.
   - ☐ c. 100 bulls are killed in the ring every year.

Score 5 points for each correct answer.

_____ **Total Score:** Recalling Facts

C Making Inferences

When you combine your own experience and information from a text to draw a conclusion that is not directly stated in that text, you are making an inference. Below are five statements that may or may not be inferences based on information in the article. Label the statements using the following key:

C—Correct Inference **F—Faulty Inference**

_______ 1. Cristina Sanchez's skill in bullfighting has totally changed the attitudes of everyone in Spain regarding whether women belong in the ring.

_______ 2. Without the examples of Juanita Cruz and Angela Hernandez to guide her, Sanchez would never have tried to become a bullfighter.

_______ 3. Cristina Sanchez is especially determined and stubborn.

_______ 4. Doing what you love, as Cristina Sanchez does, usually makes you feel happy and satisfied.

_______ 5. Bullfighting will disappear in a few years because so many people are against it.

Score 5 points for each correct answer.

_______ **Total Score:** Making Inferences

D Using Words Precisely

Each numbered sentence below contains an underlined word or phrase from the article. Following the sentence are three definitions. One definition is closest to the meaning of the underlined word. One definition is opposite or nearly opposite. Label those two definitions using the following key. Do not label the remaining definition.

C—Closest **O—Opposite or Nearly Opposite**

1. He did everything he could to <u>dissuade</u> her.

_______ a. advise not to do something

_______ b. make fun of

_______ c. talk into doing something

2. But all her father's <u>dire</u> warnings didn't scare Cristina off.

_______ a. exciting

_______ b. light-hearted

_______ c. gloomy

3. Every year hundreds of protestors gather outside the larger bullrings to <u>decry</u> the brutality of bullfighting.

_______ a. applaud

_______ b. criticize

_______ c. remember

4. "If he is a good bull, <u>combative</u> and generous in his fight, I sometimes feel badly that we have to part ways."

_______ a. strong

_______ b. peace-loving

_______ c. ready to fight

5. Cristina Sanchez has a fatalistic vision of what might happen someday.

_______ a. anxious to change the outcome

_______ b. accepting of whatever happens

_______ c. pleasant

_______ Score 3 points for each correct C answer.

_______ Score 2 points for each correct O answer.

_______ **Total Score:** Using Words Precisely

Enter the four total scores in the spaces below, and add them together to find your Reading Comprehension Score. Then record your score on the graph on page 135.

Score	Question Type	Lesson 14
_______	Finding the Main Idea	
_______	Recalling Facts	
_______	Making Inferences	
_______	Using Words Precisely	
_______	**Reading Comprehension Score**	

Author's Approach

Put an X in the box next to the correct answer.

1. What does the author mean by the statement "He [Cristina's father] went on to paint 'a black, black picture' of his own sport"?

☐ a. Cristina's father was a professional artist who often drew pictures of his sport, bullfighting.

☐ b. Cristina's father described his sport in a discouraging, negative way.

☐ c. Cristina's father thought his own sport was not worth doing.

2. Which of the following statements from the article best describes Cristina's attitude toward people who say she should not be a bullfighter?

☐ a. "'I want to make the *machistas* eat their words.'"

☐ b. "She began by fighting two-year-old bulls in small rinks."

☐ c. "Despite her supreme grace and showmanship, Cristina was still taunted by spectators."

3. What does the author imply by saying "Frustrated, she [Juanita Cruz] had all the photos and articles about her career burned just before her death in 1981"?

☐ a. Cruz was not thinking clearly just before she died.

☐ b. Cruz still felt angry and hurt when she thought about the way her dream of being a bullfighter had been destroyed.

☐ c. Someone forced Cruz to deny ever being a bullfighter.

4. Choose the statement below that best describes the author's position in paragraph 3.

☐ a. *Machistas* present a well-reasoned attitude toward female bullfighters.

☐ b. Cristina's goal of becoming a matador is silly.

☐ c. Cristina reacts bravely to opposition.

_________ Number of correct answers

Record your personal assessment of your work on the Critical Thinking Chart on page 136.

Summarizing and Paraphrasing

Put an X in the box next to the correct answer for each question.

1. Below are summaries of the article. Choose the summary that says all the most important things about the article but in the fewest words.

☐ a. Even though everyone, including her own father, discouraged her from becoming a bullfighter, Cristina Sanchez persevered and became one anyway. She has been seriously hurt in the ring, but has also showed that she has what it takes to face a fierce bull and win.

☐ b. In spite of widespread opposition, Cristina Sanchez became a bullfighter and has proved herself to be both competent and courageous.

☐ c. Cristina Sanchez followed the example of other female bullfighters and became a *matador de toros* at the age of 24.

2. Choose the best one-sentence paraphrase for the following sentence from the article:

"He knew it was a long shot that his daughter would succeed in this effort."

☐ a. He knew it was unlikely that his daughter would reach her goal.

☐ b. His daughter knew that her father did not have faith in her.

☐ c. He believed that his daughter would keep trying until she succeeded.

_________ Number of correct answers

Record your personal assessment of your work on the Critical Thinking Chart on page 136.

Critical Thinking

Put an X in the box next to the correct answer for questions 1 and 2. Follow the directions provided for questions 3 and 4.

1. Which of the following statements from the article is an opinion rather than a fact?

☐ a. "Angela? No skill, no presence…nothing."

☐ b. "At last, on May 25, 1996, Cristina Sanchez made it to the major leagues of bullfighting."

☐ c. "She graduated first in her class at the bullfighting school in Madrid."

2. From the information in paragraph 10, you can predict that Cristina will

☐ a. join those who criticize anyone for fighting bulls.

☐ b. continue to support bullfighting.

☐ c. suggest that bullfighting be made less violent.

3. Using what you know about Cristina Sanchez and what is told about Juanita Cruz in the article, name three ways Cristina Sanchez is similar to and three ways Cristina Sanchez is different from Juanita Cruz. Cite the paragraph number(s) where you found details in the article to support your conclusions.

   Similarities

   ____

   ____

   ____

   Differences

   ____

   ____

   ____

4. Think about cause-effect relationships in the article. Fill in the blanks in the cause-effect chart, drawing from the letters below.

Cause	Effect
Antonio Sanchez knew Cristina dreamed of being a matador.	____________
A law was passed prohibiting female matadors.	____________
____________	Antonio's nickname was "Scar."

   a. Juanita Cruz's career was cut short.

   b. Antonio Sanchez was gored many times

   c. Antonio Sanchez sent Cristina to a bullfighting school.

____________ Number of correct answers

Record your personal assessment of your work on the Critical Thinking Chart on page 136.

Personal Response

If I were the author, I would change

____

____

____

____

because

____

____

____

____

Self-Assessment

While reading the article, I found it easiest to

____

____

____

____

Compare and Contrast

Think about the articles you have read in Unit Two. Pick four articles that you learned the most from. Write their titles in the first column of the chart below. Use information you learned from the articles to fill in the empty boxes in the chart.

Title	What details about the activity described in this article were most interesting or new to you?	What surprised you most about this daredevil?	How does this daredevil compare with other adventurers that you knew about before reading this?

Choose the daredevil who is most unlike anyone you ever met, read about, or heard about before. Explain why you chose him or her. ________________

____

____

Words-per-Minute Table

Unit Two

Directions: If you were timed while reading an article, refer to the Reading Time you recorded in the box at the end of the article. Use this words-per-minute table to determine your reading speed for that article. Then plot your reading speed on the graph on page 134.

Lesson	8	9	10	11	12	13	14	
No. of Words	1157	1142	1078	1090	1081	962	1030	
Minutes and Seconds								*Seconds*
1:30	771	761	719	727	721	641	687	**90**
1:40	694	685	647	654	649	577	618	**100**
1:50	631	623	588	595	590	525	562	**110**
2:00	579	571	539	545	541	481	515	**120**
2:10	534	527	498	503	499	444	475	**130**
2:20	496	489	462	467	463	412	441	**140**
2:30	463	457	431	436	432	385	412	**150**
2:40	434	428	404	409	405	361	386	**160**
2:50	408	403	380	385	382	340	364	**170**
3:00	386	381	359	363	360	321	343	**180**
3:10	365	361	340	344	341	304	325	**190**
3:20	347	343	323	327	324	289	309	**200**
3:30	331	326	308	311	309	275	294	**210**
3:40	316	311	294	297	295	262	281	**220**
3:50	302	298	281	284	282	251	269	**230**
4:00	289	286	270	273	270	241	258	**240**
4:10	278	274	259	262	259	231	247	**250**
4:20	267	264	249	252	249	222	238	**260**
4:30	257	254	240	242	240	214	229	**270**
4:40	248	245	231	234	232	206	221	**280**
4:50	239	236	223	226	224	199	213	**290**
5:00	231	228	216	218	216	192	206	**300**
5:10	224	221	209	211	209	186	199	**310**
5:20	217	214	202	204	203	180	193	**320**
5:30	210	208	196	198	197	175	187	**330**
5:40	204	202	190	192	191	170	182	**340**
5:50	198	196	185	187	185	165	177	**350**
6:00	193	190	180	182	180	160	172	**360**
6:10	188	185	175	177	175	156	167	**370**
6:20	183	180	170	172	171	152	163	**380**
6:30	178	176	166	168	166	148	158	**390**
6:40	174	171	162	164	162	144	155	**400**
6:50	169	167	158	160	158	141	151	**410**
7:00	165	163	154	156	154	137	147	**420**
7:10	161	159	150	152	151	134	144	**430**
7:20	158	156	147	149	147	131	140	**440**
7:30	154	152	144	145	144	128	137	**450**
7:40	151	149	141	142	141	125	134	**460**
7:50	148	146	138	139	138	123	131	**470**
8:00	145	143	135	136	135	120	129	**480**

Plotting Your Progress: Reading Speed

Unit Two

Directions: If you were timed while reading an article, write your words-per-minute rate for that article in the box under the number of the lesson. Then plot your reading speed on the graph by putting a small X on the line directly above the number of the lesson, across from the number of words per minute you read. As you mark your speed for each lesson, graph your progress by drawing a line to connect the X's.

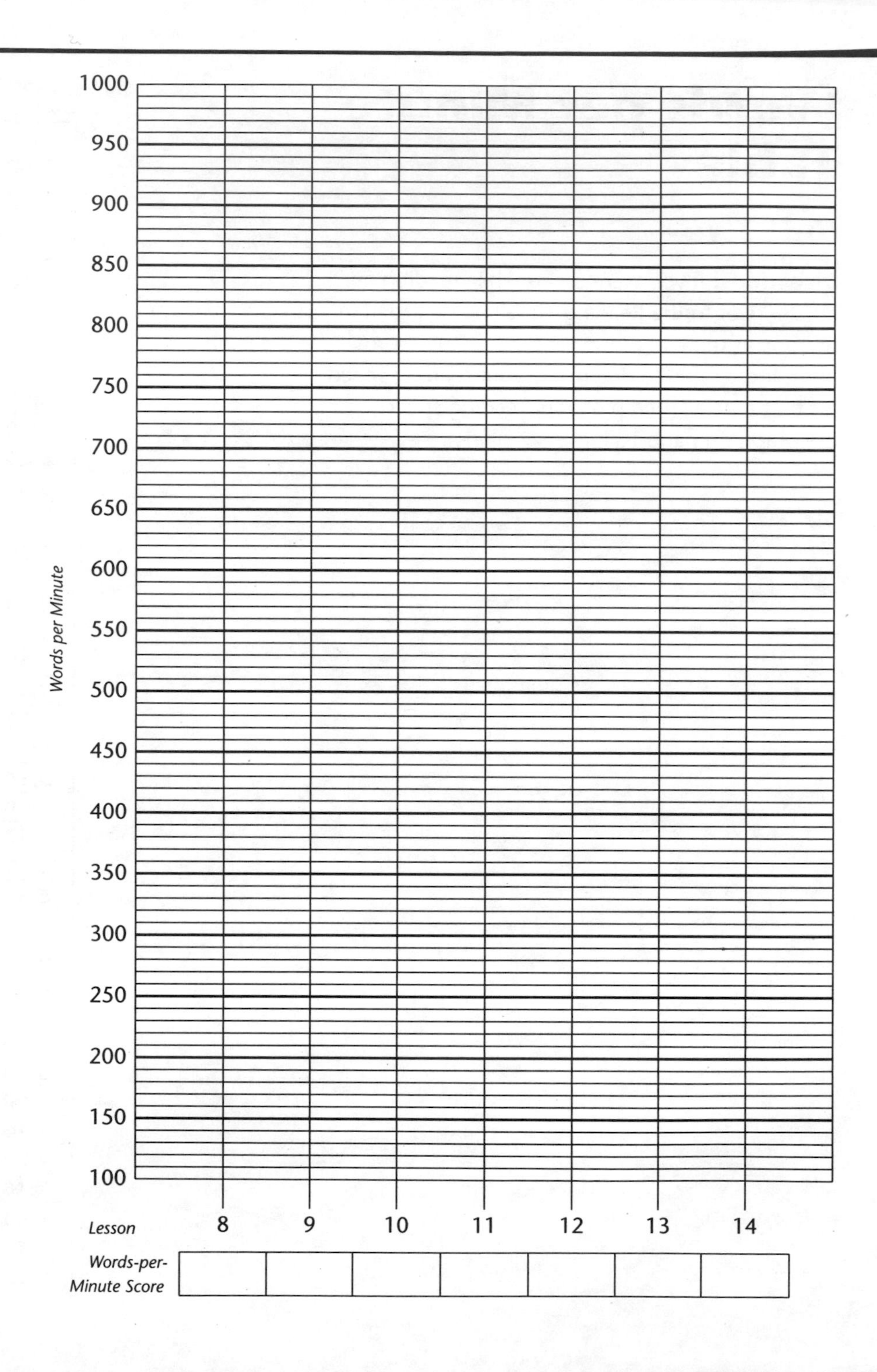

Plotting Your Progress: Reading Comprehension

Unit Two

Directions: Write your Reading Comprehension score for each lesson in the box under the number of the lesson. Then plot your score on the graph by putting a small X on the line directly above the number of the lesson and across from the score you earned. As you mark your score for each lesson, graph your progress by drawing a line to connect the X's.

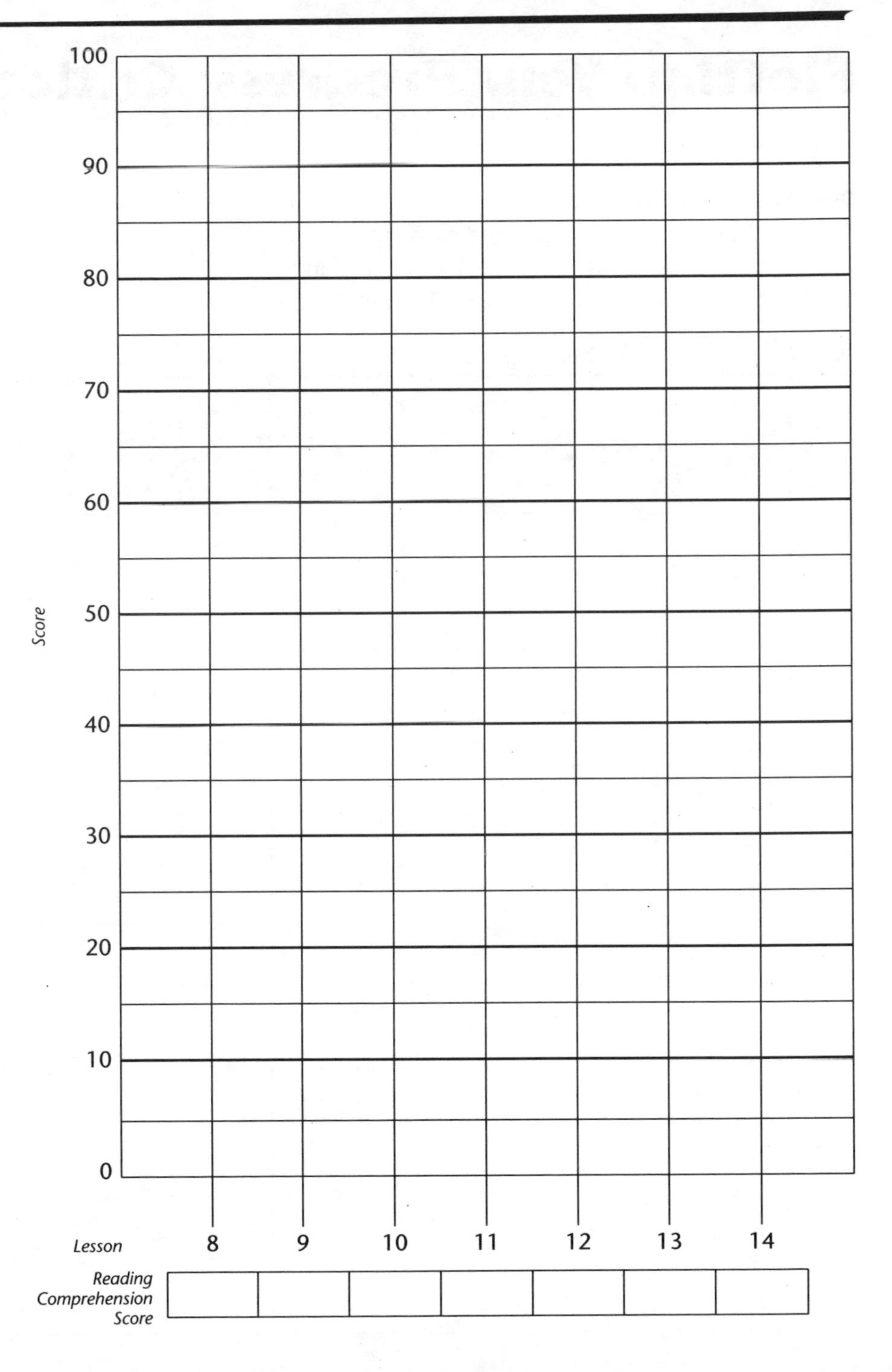

Plotting Your Progress: Critical Thinking

Unit Two

Directions: Work with your teacher to evaluate your responses to the Critical Thinking questions for each lesson. Then fill in the appropriate spaces in the chart below. For each lesson and each type of Critical Thinking question, do the following: Mark a minus sign (–) in the box to indicate areas in which you feel you could improve. Mark a plus sign (+) to indicate areas in which you feel you did well. Mark a minus-slash-plus sign (–/+) to indicate areas in which you had mixed success. Then write any comments you have about your performance, including ideas for improvement.

Lesson	Author's Approach	Summarizing and Paraphrasing	Critical Thinking
8			
9			
10			
11			
12			
13			
14			

UNIT THREE

OPERATION DESERT HELL

Fighting Oil Well Fires

A safety engineer once asked Red Adair to take off his tin helmet and wear a plastic safety helmet instead. It was a regulation, the engineer insisted. Adair tried to explain that the work he and his firefighters did was far too hot for plastic helmets, but the engineer wouldn't listen. At last, Adair suggested that the engineer put on the plastic helmet himself and accompany Adair on a short walk.

2 "I took that dude down as close to the fire as he could stand it and stood there with him," Adair said. "The brim of that plastic hat of his started to melt." Added Adair, "I think he began to get an idea of how hot a well fire can be."

3 The safety engineer should have listened to Adair in the first place. Adair knew more about fighting oil well fires than anyone else. Over his long career, Paul "Red" Adair had "killed" oil well fires all over the globe. In 1962, he capped a burning Algerian well known as "The Devil's Cigarette Lighter." In 1970, he extinguished a massive blaze off the coast of Louisiana. And in 1988, he conquered a raging inferno in the North Sea. Whenever there was trouble in an oil field, the

At the end of the Gulf War, Iraqi troops ignited oil well fires in Kuwait. Here, firefighters from 4 different companies battle the fires.

word went out: "Get Red Adair, and get him quick."

4 Battling oil well fires is among the most hazardous occupations in the world. The heat from such a blaze can reach 4,000 degrees Fahrenheit. When a firefighter approaches a burning well, the soles of his shoes may begin to blister and the cuffs of his pants may smoke. Adair once had a credit card melt in his pocket. As Larry Arnold, a member of Adair's firefighting crew, said, "When you smell your moustache burning, you know you're too close."

5 Over the years, Red Adair and his crew put out dozens of seemingly unstoppable oil well fires. Then, in 1991, the Persian Gulf War resulted in a challenge that made all previous fires seem like child's play. Earlier, the nation of Iraq had invaded and conquered its tiny oil-rich neighbor, Kuwait. The United States and other nations responded by driving the Iraqis out of Kuwait in Operation Desert Storm.

6 Before leaving Kuwait, however, the Iraqis ignited over 500 oil wells. These fires burned more than six million barrels of oil a day. Crude oil was going up in flames at a rate of a $1,000 a second! The black smoke was so dense it blotted out the noonday sun and fouled the atmosphere as far away as Hawaii. It seemed as if the whole nation was on fire. Dave Wilson, an engineer in Kuwait, said at the time, "You half expect to see little guys with pitchforks and tails coming out of the ground."

7 It was little wonder that the task of extinguishing these fires came to be known as Operation Desert Hell. The job was far too big for the 75-year-old Red Adair and his company alone, so three other firefighting companies joined the effort. These companies were Boots & Coots and Wild Well Control from Texas and Safety Boss from Canada.

8 Nobody had ever seen a situation quite like this one. There was nothing but fire, smoke, and sticky pools of oil all over the place. Desert winds blowing 50 miles per hour fanned the flames of the burning wells. With so much oil around, any random spark could ignite a fire. One day two journalists got their car stuck in a pool of oil. Three other men, who had been driving a water truck, stopped to help out. Without warning, the oil caught fire, blowing up both vehicles and killing all the men. The searing heat consumed just about everything. Rescuers found only a set of leg bones, a charred spinal column, and a skull fused to the springs of the car seat.

9 Danger lurked everywhere in the overpowering heat of the Kuwaiti desert. The burning wells and pools of oil were obvious dangers, but there were other hazards as well. Kuwait had been ground zero in the Persian Gulf War. Iraqi soldiers had planted mines in the Kuwaiti desert, while the United States and its allies had

Oil well firefighter Red Adair

dropped bombs. Some of the mines still remained, and some of the bombs hadn't exploded when they hit the ground. Now these deadly devices were completely covered with oil. One day a camel stepped on one, blowing itself to pieces. "Every day I'm in [the] field," joked one firefighter, "I find three or four new ways to die." Candy-striped tape was used to identify those parts of the desert that had been cleared of mines and bombs. Anyone who walked elsewhere could end up like the camel.

10 Killing an oil well fire requires patience as well as courage. When a well has been burning for a while, the super-hot blaze of burning oil creates a lava-hard mound of "coke" around the wellhead. The mound has to be knocked down to expose the wellhead. This task is accomplished with a tractor equipped with a 70-foot boom that scrapes away at the mound. It sometimes take several hours to find a weak spot in the mound. When the mound finally collapses, the well explodes with shattering force. Clearly, it takes guts to operate a tractor so close to the well.

11 Once the wellhead is exposed, the fire can be snuffed out either by drowning it with torrents of water or by dropping dynamite on it. Many of the Kuwaiti wells were simply too hot to be killed with water alone. They required blasting. Once the fire is extinguished, however, the most fearful part begins. At that point, oil is still spraying out of the well. To stop the spray, firefighters must get to the well and cap it, knowing that at any moment the tiniest spark or wind-blown ember could cause the fumes in the air to "flash," or burst into flames, killing them all.

12 On ordinary jobs there is only one fire to extinguish, but the problem in Kuwait was different. "On another job you've only got one fire," explained Coots Matthews of Coots & Boots. "On this one you just go on to another well."

13 The job of killing and capping more than 500 raging well fires began early in March of 1991. It took the firefighters eight grueling months to finish the job. The total cost to Kuwait was estimated to be in excess of $5 billion. And the precious oil resources that the Iraqis so senselessly burned were lost forever. Still, without the determination and skill of the oil well firefighters, the cost would have been much, much higher.

If you have been timed while reading this article, enter your reading time below. Then turn to the Words-per-Minute Table on page 195 and look up your reading speed (words per minute). Enter your reading speed on the graph on page 196.

Reading Time: Lesson 15

_______ : _______

Minutes *Seconds*

A Finding the Main Idea

One statement below expresses the main idea of the article. One statement is too general, or too broad. The other statement explains only part of the article; it is too narrow. Label the statements using the following key:

M—Main Idea **B—Too Broad** **N—Too Narrow**

______ 1. Trained oil well firefighters bravely fought the oil well fires that the Iraqis ignited as they left Kuwait.

______ 2. In Kuwait, oil well blazes were burning more than six million barrels of oil per day at a rate of $1,000 per second.

______ 3. The task of fighting fires must be faced every day in every country on the face of the globe.

______ Score 15 points for a correct M answer.

______ Score 5 points for each correct B or N answer.

______ **Total Score:** Finding the Main Idea

B Recalling Facts

How well do you remember the facts in the article? Put an X in the box next to the answer that correctly completes each statement about the article.

1. In addition to fighting the Kuwait oil well fires, Red Adair had battled oil well fires in the
   - ☐ a. ocean off Louisiana.
   - ☐ b. Gobi Desert.
   - ☐ c. Antarctic Ocean.

2. Iraqis set the oil wells on fire at the close of the
   - ☐ a. Korean War.
   - ☐ b. Persian Gulf War.
   - ☐ c. 1990 Olympic Games.

3. In addition to fighting fires, firefighters had to be careful to avoid
   - ☐ a. camels.
   - ☐ b. lightning strikes.
   - ☐ c. buried mines and unexploded bombs.

4. The two main ways of killing an oil well fire mentioned in the article are
   - ☐ a. pouring a synthetic chemical on it and covering it with dirt.
   - ☐ b. covering it with dirt and drowning it with water.
   - ☐ c. drowning it with water and dropping dynamite down it.

5. To extinguish all the oil well fires in Kuwait took
   - ☐ a. two years.
   - ☐ b. eight months.
   - ☐ c. six weeks.

Score 5 points for each correct answer.

______ **Total Score:** Recalling Facts

C Making Inferences

When you combine your own experience and information from a text to draw a conclusion that is not directly stated in that text, you are making an inference. Below are five statements that may or may not be inferences based on information in the article. Label the statements using the following key:

C—Correct Inference **F—Faulty Inference**

_______ 1. The safety engineer who insisted that Adair wear a plastic helmet had never battled an oil well fire.

_______ 2. There are only a few qualified oil well firefighters in the world.

_______ 3. The smoke from even a huge fire can travel only a few hundred miles.

_______ 4. Only men are allowed to battle oil well fires.

_______ 5. People who fight oil well fires should wear flameproof protective clothing.

Score 5 points for each correct answer.

_______ **Total Score:** Making Inferences

D Using Words Precisely

Each numbered sentence below contains an underlined word or phrase from the article. Following the sentence are three definitions. One definition is closest to the meaning of the underlined word. One definition is opposite or nearly opposite. Label those two definitions using the following key. Do not label the remaining definition.

C—Closest **O—Opposite or Nearly Opposite**

1. And in 1988, he conquered a raging <u>inferno</u> in the North Sea.

_______ a. small, easily controlled flame

_______ b. problem

_______ c. huge, intense fire

2. Battling oil well fires is among the most <u>hazardous</u> occupations in the world.

_______ a. popular

_______ b. dangerous

_______ c. safe

3. The black smoke was so dense it blotted out the noonday sun and <u>fouled</u> the atmosphere as far away as Hawaii.

_______ a. dirtied

_______ b. dried out

_______ c. cleaned

4. It took the firefighters eight <u>grueling</u> months to finish the job.

_______ a. hungry

_______ b. painless

_______ c. difficult and exhausting

5. The total cost to Kuwait was estimated to be in excess of $5 billion.

_______ a. less than

_______ b. more than

_______ c. unbelievably

_______ Score 3 points for each correct C answer.

_______ Score 2 points for each correct O answer.

_______ **Total Score:** Using Words Precisely

Enter the four total scores in the spaces below, and add them together to find your Reading Comprehension Score. Then record your score on the graph on page 197.

Score	Question Type	Lesson 15
_______	Finding the Main Idea	
_______	Recalling Facts	
_______	Making Inferences	
_______	Using Words Precisely	
_______	**Reading Comprehension Score**	

Author's Approach

Put an X in the box next to the correct answer.

1. Judging by statements from the article "Operation Desert Hell: Fighting Oil Well Fires," you can conclude that the author wants the reader to think that

☐ a. the Iraqis were irresponsible in setting the oil well fires in Kuwait.

☐ b. oil well firefighters are braver than ordinary firefighters.

☐ c. Red Adair was too old to fight the fires in Kuwait alone.

2. How is the author's purpose for writing the article expressed in paragraph 13?

☐ a. The paragraph informs the reader of the cost of the fires.

☐ b. The paragraph tells how long the fires lasted.

☐ c. The paragraph tells about the fires and praises the firefighters.

3. The author probably wrote this article in order to

☐ a. express an opinion about war.

☐ b. entertain the reader with a humorous story.

☐ c. inform the reader about dangerous fires and the people who bravely fought them.

_______ Number of correct answers

Record your personal assessment of your work on the Critical Thinking Chart on page 198.

Summarizing and Paraphrasing

Follow the directions provided for questions 1 and 2. Put an X in the box next to the correct answer for question 3.

1. Complete the following one-sentence summary of the article using the lettered phrases from the phrase bank below. Write the letters on the lines.

Phrase Bank:

a. a description of Red Adair's early experiences in putting out oil well fires
b. how the firefighters finally extinguished the Kuwait fires
c. the situation the firefighters faced in Kuwait

After a short introduction, the article "Operation Desert Hell: Fighting Oil Well Fires" begins with ________, goes on to explain________, and ends with________.

2. Reread paragraph 3 in the article. Below, write a summary of the paragraph in no more than 25 words.

____

____

____

____

Reread your summary and decide whether it covers the important ideas in the paragraph. Next, decide how to shorten the summary to 15 words or less without leaving out any essential information. Write this summary below.

____

____

3. Choose the sentence that correctly restates the following sentence from the article:

"Kuwait had been ground zero in the Persian Gulf War."

☐ a. Buildings in Kuwait were knocked down to the ground during the Persian Gulf War.
☐ b. Kuwait had been extremely cold during the Persian Gulf War.
☐ c. Most of the action of the Persian Gulf War took place in Kuwait.

________ Number of correct answers

Record your personal assessment of your work on the Critical Thinking Chart on page 198.

Critical Thinking

Follow the directions provided for questions 1, 2, and 5. Put an X in the box next to the correct answer for questions 3 and 4.

1. Choose from the letters below to correctly complete the following statement. Write the letters on the lines.

On the positive side, ________, but on the negative side ________.

a. candy-striped tape was used to identify areas that had been cleared of bombs and mines
b. precious oil reserves were lost
c. the firefighters were successful in putting out the Kuwait fires

CRITICAL THINKING

2. Think about cause-effect relationships in the article. Fill in the blanks in the cause-effect chart, drawing from the letters below.

Cause	Effect
The Iraqis invaded Kuwait.	________
The oil well fires were too hot.	________
________	It blew itself to pieces.

a. The United States and other nations drove the Iraqis out.

b. A camel stepped on a mine.

c. They had to be blasted to be extinguished.

3. Of the following theme categories, which would this story fit into?

☐ a. adventure

☐ b. romance

☐ c. humor

4. If you were a beginning oil well firefighter, how could you use the information in the article to put out an oil well fire?

☐ a. You could remember not to take any plastic credit cards near an oil well fire.

☐ b. You could learn that you can put out an oil well fire by drowning it with massive amounts of water or by dropping dynamite down it.

☐ c. You could give the fires exciting names, like the firefighters in the article did.

5. Which paragraphs from the article provide evidence that supports your answer to question 2?

____

________ Number of correct answers

Record your personal assessment of your work on the Critical Thinking Chart on page 198.

Personal Response

What was most surprising or interesting to you about this article?

____

____

____

____

Self-Assessment

A word or phrase in the article that I do not understand is

____

____

____

____

LESSON 16

PICABO STREET
Fearless Skier

People used to laugh at her because of her funny name—it's pronounced like the name of a game you play with babies: peek-a-boo. But when Picabo Street steps into her skis and heads down the slope, the laughter stops and the murmurs of admiration begin. Anyone who has ever seen her race can tell you that Picabo Street is one of the most electrifying women the world of skiing has ever seen.

2 It's not just that Picabo is a fast skier; it's that she is *fearless*. She attacks the slopes with an energy and confidence that send shivers down the spines of spectators and fellow racers alike. She has been clocked flying down mountains at close to 80 miles per hour. Her all-out style has led the Swiss to nickname her "One Crazy Red Hen." The Austrians call her "The Freckle-Faced Jet Fighter Pilot."

3 Some of the credit for Picabo's fearlessness goes to her parents, Dee and Stubby. They gave their daughter an unconventional childhood in hopes it would make her strong and independent. When Picabo was an infant, for instance, her parents decided not to give her a name. They wanted her to pick her own name when she got old enough to do so. For two years, her official title was "Baby Girl Street." Her name was finally changed only because the family needed passports for a trip to Mexico, and passport officials would not issue one to a child without a name. Dee and Stubby chose "Picabo" because their daughter liked to play peek-a-boo. They took the unusual spelling of the word from the name of a town in Idaho named for a nearby river. In the local Native American language, *picabo* means "shining water."

Olympic medalist Picabo Street streaks downhill on her way to winning another championship.

4 As Picabo grew older, her parents encouraged her to be self-reliant and to face every challenge that came her way. In their tiny mountain community of Triumph, Idaho, Picabo learned to chop wood, raise hens, and grow her own food. The Streets had no television, so Picabo entertained herself by doing bicycle tricks, playing tackle football, and having boxing matches with the boys in the neighborhood.

5 When Picabo was six, her father introduced her to skiing. He took her up the big slopes at Sun Valley. "He used to make me chase him down the mountain," she says. "That's how I learned to ski fast."

6 Ultimately, of course, Dee and Stubby's encouragement could only take Picabo so far. To become a world champion downhill skier, she had to find the desire within herself. At first it looked as though she couldn't go wrong. By the age of ten, she was entering ski races and beating everyone in sight, including girls who were much older. And in 1989, when she was just 17, she made the U.S. Ski Team.

7 But while Picabo had plenty of talent, she didn't yet have much discipline. Her parents had succeeded in getting her to question rules—but now the rules she was questioning were the rules of the U.S. Ski Team. She balked at the idea of following

Picabo Street with her parents, Roland and Dee

the team schedule. She didn't like coaches deciding when she would train and how she would train. "I didn't want someone telling me what to do all the time," she says.

8 Her attitude bothered many of the trainers, who found her lazy and quarrelsome. Said one trainer, "She'll never win. She can't follow the rules."

9 Coach Paul Major saw the situation differently. "That's why she *will* win," he responded.

10 Major had followed Picabo's career for three years. He had seen her rise through the ranks of amateurs to win a place on his American team. He believed she had the potential to be one of the greatest skiers ever. He liked her aggressive, unorthodox style. But even he saw that she needed to accept certain rules. He said, "Picabo burst onto the ski team with natural talent. She threw herself down the hill. No obstacles. But she relied on natural talent to keep her on the team. She didn't know the stakes had been raised. She didn't push herself. She wasn't conditioned well enough. She was rebelling, asking why she should conform." When Picabo failed to do the exercises needed to condition her body properly, Major did what he had to do. He kicked Picabo Street off the U.S. team.

11 For several weeks, Picabo stumbled around at loose ends. She didn't know what she wanted to do with her life. When her parents heard what had happened, Stubby gave her two choices. She could come home and begin serious training under his supervision, or she could be cut loose from the family and go her own way. Picabo decided to come home.

12 For three months Stubby kept her on a strict regimen of sit-ups, push-ups, swimming, and running. That was enough to put her back on the team. Still, Picabo had a long way to go to earn the respect of her teammates and coaches. But as she had done so often in her life, Picabo rose to the challenge. In 1991 and 1992, she won the American Championship Series. In 1993, she captured a silver medal at the world championships. The next year she took a silver medal at the Olympic Games. And after that, she walked away with two World Cup downhill titles. She was the first U.S. skier, male or female, to win that title.

13 As she blew by the competition in race after race, Picabo proved that she really is one of the best skiers ever. She is also one of the most popular. Fans love to watch her streak down the hill at top speeds, holding nothing back. She is fast, she is graceful, and she shows just enough recklessness to thrill the crowds. As Coach Paul Major put it, "there's just a touch there that few skiers have."

14 Picabo herself puts it this way, "This sport does define me. It's pretty intense in speed, in concentration, and in focus. Downhill is graceful, like a dance. I like to make it flowing so people enjoy watching me. You also need to be fearless. I'll jump off a 60-foot cliff into water, and not just because someone's goading me."

If you have been timed while reading this article, enter your reading time below. Then turn to the Words-per-Minute Table on page 195 and look up your reading speed (words per minute). Enter your reading speed on the graph on page 196.

Reading Time: Lesson 16

________ : ________

Minutes *Seconds*

A Finding the Main Idea

One statement below expresses the main idea of the article. One statement is too general, or too broad. The other statement explains only part of the article; it is too narrow. Label the statements using the following key:

M—Main Idea **B—Too Broad** **N—Too Narrow**

_______ 1. Picabo Street is a fast and fearless skier who attacks her sport with both discipline and enthusiasm.

_______ 2. To excel in most sports, athletes must accept strict discipline and show a willingness to follow the rules.

_______ 3. When skiing great Picabo Street was only 17, she was invited to be part of the U.S. Ski Team.

_______ Score 15 points for a correct M answer.

_______ Score 5 points for each correct B or N answer.

_______ **Total Score:** Finding the Main Idea

B Recalling Facts

How well do you remember the facts in the article? Put an X in the box next to the answer that correctly completes each statement about the article.

1. Until Picabo Street was two years old, she was called
- ☐ a. Baby Girl.
- ☐ b. Stubby.
- ☐ c. Dee.

2. Street was introduced to skiing
- ☐ a. near her home in Norway.
- ☐ b. in Switzerland.
- ☐ c. at Sun Valley, Idaho.

3. One of her trainers said that Street couldn't win because she
- ☐ a. wasn't strong enough.
- ☐ b. couldn't follow the rules.
- ☐ c. just wasn't fast enough.

4. After Street refused to do the exercises her coach told her to do,
- ☐ a. she fell during the next race.
- ☐ b. he kicked her off the team.
- ☐ c. her coach agreed that she really didn't need to follow the rules.

5. In the 1994 Olympics, Picabo Street won a
- ☐ a. bronze medal.
- ☐ b. silver medal.
- ☐ c. gold medal.

Score 5 points for each correct answer.

_______ **Total Score:** Recalling Facts

C Making Inferences

When you combine your own experience and information from a text to draw a conclusion that is not directly stated in that text, you are making an inference. Below are five statements that may or may not be inferences based on information in the article. Label the statements using the following key:

C—Correct Inference **F—Faulty Inference**

_______ 1. When children are raised in a slightly unusual way, they are likely to become star athletes.

_______ 2. It is not necessary for young children from the United States to get passports when they travel to foreign countries.

_______ 3. Picabo Street was blessed with good health for much of her childhood.

_______ 4. When you have enough natural talent, you don't need to do any conditioning exercises.

_______ 5. No Americans had entered the World Cup competition before the years in which Street won the title.

Score 5 points for each correct answer.

_______ **Total Score:** Making Inferences

D Using Words Precisely

Each numbered sentence below contains an underlined word or phrase from the article. Following the sentence are three definitions. One definition is closest to the meaning of the underlined word. One definition is opposite or nearly opposite. Label those two definitions using the following key. Do not label the remaining definition.

C—Closest **O—Opposite or Nearly Opposite**

1. They gave their daughter an unconventional childhood in hopes it would make her strong and independent.

_______ a. normal

_______ b. out of the ordinary

_______ c. easy

2. She balked at the idea of following the team schedule.

_______ a. resisted

_______ b. gladly accepted

_______ c. played with

3. He had seen her rise through the ranks of amateurs to win a place on his American team.

_______ a. people who take part in a sport as a profession

_______ b. people who take part in a sport but don't really enjoy it

_______ c. people who take part in a sport without being paid

4. He liked her aggressive, unorthodox style.

_______ a. not according to usual customs

_______ b. traditional

_______ c. proud

5. "I'll jump off a 60-foot cliff into water, and not just because someone's goading me."

_______ a. discouraging

_______ b. kidding

_______ c. urging

_______ Score 3 points for each correct C answer.

_______ Score 2 points for each correct O answer.

_______ **Total Score:** Using Words Precisely

Enter the four total scores in the spaces below, and add them together to find your Reading Comprehension Score. Then record your score on the graph on page 197.

Score	Question Type	Lesson 16
_______	Finding the Main Idea	
_______	Recalling Facts	
_______	Making Inferences	
_______	Using Words Precisely	
_______	**Reading Comprehension Score**	

Author's Approach

Put an X in the box next to the correct answer.

1. The author uses the first sentence of the article to

☐ a. inform the reader about how to say Picabo Street's name.

☐ b. describe the qualities of Picabo Street

☐ c. express an opinion about Picabo Street.

2. Which of the following statements from the article best describes the way Picabo Street skied?

☐ a. "Fans love to watch her streak down the hill at top speeds, holding nothing back."

☐ b. "Her attitude bothered many of the trainers, who found her lazy and quarrelsome."

☐ c. "For three months Stubby kept her on a strict regimen of sit-ups, push-ups, swimming, and running."

3. Choose the statement below that best describes the author's position in paragraph 12.

☐ a. Picabo Street belonged on the U.S. Ski Team and shouldn't have been cut.

☐ b. Picabo Street is a hard-working competitor who rises to every challenge.

☐ c. The fact that Street won the World Cup downhill title proves that she is the best skier in history.

4. The author tells this story mainly by

☐ a. telling events in the order they happened.

☐ b. comparing different topics.

☐ c. using his or her imagination and creativity.

_______ Number of correct answers

Record your personal assessment of your work on the Critical Thinking Chart on page 198.

Summarizing and Paraphrasing

Follow the directions provided for question 1. Put an X in the box next to the correct answer for the other question.

1. Look for the important ideas and events in paragraphs 7 and 8. Summarize those paragraphs in one or two sentences.

____

____

____

2. Read the statement about the article below. Then read the paraphrase of that statement. Choose the reason that best tells why the paraphrase does not say the same thing as the statement.

   Statement: Picabo Street was not used to following anyone else's rules.

   Paraphrase: After her somewhat unorthodox childhood, Picabo Street was not accustomed to conforming to rules another person created, and so she refused to do the exercises her coach ordered.

☐ a. Paraphrase says too much.

☐ b. Paraphrase doesn't say enough.

☐ c. Paraphrase doesn't agree with the statement about the article.

_______ Number of correct answers

Record your personal assessment of your work on the Critical Thinking Chart on page 198.

Critical Thinking

Follow the directions provided for questions 1, 3, and 4. Put an X in the box next to the correct answer for question 2.

1. For each statement below, write O if it expresses an opinion or write F if it expresses a fact.

_______ a. Picabo Street is an electrifying skier.

_______ b. The Swiss call Street "One Crazy Red Hen."

_______ c. Picabo Street won the American Championship Series in 1991 and 1992.

2. Considering Picabo Street's actions as described in this article, you can predict that she will

☐ a. give up skiing to try a different sport.

☐ b. continue to ski as long as possible.

☐ c. become too nervous to try anything dangerous.

3. Choose from the letters below to correctly complete the following statement. Write the letters on the lines.

   According to the article, _______ caused Coach Major to _______, and the effect was _______.

   a. Street's refusal to exercise

   b. Street decided to train under her father's supervision

   c. cut Street from the team

CRITICAL THINKING

4. Which paragraphs from the article provide evidence that supports your answer to question 3?

____

_____ Number of correct answers

Record your personal assessment of your work on the Critical Thinking Chart on page 198.

Personal Response

Begin the first 5–8 sentences of your own article about downhill skiing. It may tell of a real experience or one that is imagined.

____

____

____

____

____

____

Self-Assessment

One of the things I did best when reading this article was

____

____

____

____

I believe I did this well because

____

____

____

____

LESSON 17

ELEPHANT KEEPERS

When you look at lions or tigers in the zoo, you may imagine that if they could get their claws on you, they'd rip you to pieces. Elephants, on the other hand, seem less threatening. Sure, they're big, but they are also slow and lumbering and seem perfectly content to be led around by their keepers. Don't let their seemingly sweet dispositions fool you, however. Every now and then, elephants do get mad. And when they do, they'll trample, crush, or stomp anyone in sight. Usually that "anyone" is one of their keepers or trainers. Every year, unfortunate elephant handlers find themselves at the mercy of raging beasts weighing 10,000 pounds or more.

2 If you don't believe it, just ask the people who worked with Tyke. In 1973, this 20-year-old female African elephant was on tour with the Great American Circus. One day she became agitated during a performance in Pennsylvania. She charged through the arena, terrorizing the 3,000 children in the stands. Her trainers managed to calm her down before anyone was injured.

3 Two months later, however, at the North Dakota State Fair, her handlers were

An elephant keeper bathes one of the elephants at the Bronx Zoo.

not so lucky. No one knows what set Tyke off that day, but for some reason she pulled away from trainer Tyrone Taylor. She ran right over groomer Mike Pursely, crushing three of his ribs. For 25 minutes she stormed through the midway while trainers and sheriffs chased after her. Finally, she was brought under control.

4 But the following year her temper erupted again in Honolulu, Hawaii. This time it was trainer Allen Campbell and groomer Dallas Beckwith who happened to be in her path. Beckwith was badly injured by the stampeding elephant, as were several spectators. Campbell was crushed to death. After she trampled the men, Tyke took off on a rampage. As she thundered through the streets of the city, police pursued her with their guns drawn. It took 89 bullets to bring her down.

5 After Campbell's death, Tony Vecchio, director of Rhode Island's Roger Williams Zoo, went on record saying he didn't think zoos should keep elephants at all. "The guy who I thought was the best elephant trainer in the world, Allen Campbell, was killed in Hawaii," said Vecchio. "If he could be killed by an elephant, I don't think any keeper could be safe." Vecchio pointed out that elephants "can kill you in a second, and there's nothing you can do to stop them." He added, "They're the most dangerous animal in the zoo business."

6 There are many examples to back up Vecchio's words. In 1991, an elephant keeper in England thought his elephant's foot looked sore. As he tried to examine it, the elephant lowered her head and butted the man. The force of her blow knocked him against the bars of the cage, snapping his neck and killing him. That same year, a California elephant keeper was kicked to death as he tried to clean out his elephant's pen. The next year, it was Texas where an elephant grabbed her keeper with her trunk and killed him by smashing his body against the ground. And the year after that, an elephant at a Florida zoo killed her handler by knocking him down with her trunk and then kicking him as hard as she could.

7 To be fair to the elephants, you'd have to admit that they do sometimes have reasons for their fits of rage. Consider the case of a female elephant who was raised in an El Salvador zoo without a mate. For elephants, who are naturally social creatures, this kind of life could lead only to great unhappiness. After 15 years, the elephant finally snapped. As horrified school children looked on, she crushed her keeper to death.

8 At a wildlife park in Belgium, keepers made a similar mistake. They separated a male elephant and his mate, putting the two in different pens. Furious, both elephants broke free and trampled one keeper to death.

9 It was despair, not fury, that sent a Houston elephant over the edge. After a typical 20-month pregnancy, the elephant gave birth to a live baby, called a calf. The newborn didn't last long, though, and the mother elephant watched her little calf

An elephant keeper at the San Diego Zoo gives an Asian elephant a treat for a job well done.

die. For the next two months the mother seemed alternately depressed and angry. One day, she went crazy and attacked her trainer, breaking his collarbone and four of his ribs.

10 At the Cleveland Zoo, an elephant went berserk over a different problem. In January 1994, Cleveland was hit with a deep cold spell. Temperatures stayed below zero for days. It was too cold to take the elephants out for exercise; they had to be confined to their cages. One elephant apparently couldn't tolerate the confinement. When her keeper came to visit her, she lunged at him, gashing his head with her tusk.

11 Sometimes elephants are startled by some loud or sudden noise. In Spain, a 1993 parade ended in tragedy when a dog began to bark. The elephant who was leading the parade grew frightened and gored his handler in the back, killing the man. In Florida, it was the noise of a car that surprised an elephant, causing her to trample and kill her handler.

12 Then there was the case of Calle, a 30-year-old Asian elephant at the Los Angeles Zoo. On October 20, 1996, Calle spent the afternoon in the usual way. She performed her training drills in front of dozens of curious spectators. But near the end of the day, a journalist began snapping flash photographs of her. Again and again, the camera's light bulb popped in front of Calle's eyes. In response, Calle picked up a small rock with her trunk and threw it at the man's head. She also threw a clump of dirt at him. Said zookeeper Susie Kasielke, "She's being rude, just like an eight-year-old child." But shortly after that, Calle stepped on keeper Ronald Rutter, breaking three of his ribs and shattering his collarbone.

13 The dangers of working with elephants has not escaped the notice of zoo owners. In the wake of so many injuries and deaths, some owners have adopted new policies that try to minimize human contact with elephants. Still, such contact cannot be completely avoided. Where lions and tigers can be left pretty much on their own, elephants need daily care by humans. They need baths to keep their skin healthy. They also need to be brushed to keep dead skin from building up on their bodies. They need their toenails clipped to keep their feet in good shape. All these tasks require humans to work in close contact with them.

14 But it isn't just necessity that keeps elephant handlers close to their animals. Keepers and trainers say they enjoy working with elephants. They love the challenge of caring for such intelligent creatures. In addition to physical care, they provide their elephants with mental stimulation. They also make sure their social needs are being met. Despite the risks, many elephant trainers regard their elephants as good friends. In 1993, trainer Alex Gautier summed up the feelings of many trainers. Referring to the 21 elephants he looks after, he said, "They're part of my family."

If you have been timed while reading this article, enter your reading time below. Then turn to the Words-per-Minute Table on page 195 and look up your reading speed (words per minute). Enter your reading speed on the graph on page 196.

Reading Time: Lesson 17

______ : ______

Minutes *Seconds*

A Finding the Main Idea

One statement below expresses the main idea of the article. One statement is too general, or too broad. The other statement explains only part of the article; it is too narrow. Label the statements using the following key:

M—Main Idea **B—Too Broad** **N—Too Narrow**

_____ 1. A circus elephant named Tyke one day went crazy and charged at children in the audience before she was brought under control.

_____ 2. Elephants are not always popular with zoo owners for a variety of reasons.

_____ 3. Though elephants look calm and sweet, they are known to launch into fits of rage in which they injure or kill their trainers and handlers.

_____ Score 15 points for a correct M answer.

_____ Score 5 points for each correct B or N answer.

_____ **Total Score:** Finding the Main Idea

B Recalling Facts

How well do you remember the facts in the article? Put an X in the box next to the answer that correctly completes each statement about the article.

1. An elephant named Tyke ran out of control through
   - ☐ a. Cleveland, Ohio.
   - ☐ b. Honolulu, Hawaii.
   - ☐ c. San Antonio, Texas.
2. Tyke killed her trainer
   - ☐ a. Allen Campbell.
   - ☐ b. Tony Vecchio.
   - ☐ c. Ronald Rutter.
3. An elephant in an El Salvador zoo went berserk because
   - ☐ a. her mate had died.
   - ☐ b. she didn't like her mate.
   - ☐ c. she had been without a mate for 15 years.
4. A Houston elephant who bore a calf was depressed because
   - ☐ a. the calf soon died.
   - ☐ b. the zookeepers took the calf away.
   - ☐ c. the calf refused to have anything to do with its mother.
5. Elephants need humans to do all these tasks except
   - ☐ a. polish their tusks.
   - ☐ b. give them baths.
   - ☐ c. cut their toenails.

Score 5 points for each correct answer.

_____ **Total Score:** Recalling Facts

C Making Inferences

When you combine your own experience and information from a text to draw a conclusion that is not directly stated in that text, you are making an inference. Below are five statements that may or may not be inferences based on information in the article. Label the statements using the following key:

C—Correct Inference **F—Faulty Inference**

_______ 1. Soon there will be no elephants in zoos because they are too difficult to take care of.

_______ 2. People who work with elephants should undergo thorough training.

_______ 3. Elephants in the wild never become angry or go berserk, as they do in zoos and circuses.

_______ 4. Elephants are easier to upset than any other animal.

_______ 5. In the wild, elephants like to live in groups.

Score 5 points for each correct answer.

_______ **Total Score:** Making Inferences

D Using Words Precisely

Each numbered sentence below contains an underlined word or phrase from the article. Following the sentence are three definitions. One definition is closest to the meaning of the underlined word. One definition is opposite or nearly opposite. Label those two definitions using the following key. Do not label the remaining definition.

C—Closest **O—Opposite or Nearly Opposite**

1. Sure, they're big, but they are also slow and <u>lumbering</u> and seem perfectly content to be led around by their keepers.

_______ a. clumsy

_______ b. kind

_______ c. graceful

2. One day she became <u>agitated</u> during a performance in Pennsylvania.

_______ a. calm

_______ b. excited

_______ c. curious

3. But the following year her temper <u>erupted</u> again in Honolulu, Hawaii.

_______ a. fought

_______ b. flared up

_______ c. died down

4. As <u>horrified</u> school children looked on, she crushed her keeper to death.

_______ a. happy

_______ b. escaping

_______ c. terrified

5. At the Cleveland Zoo, an elephant went berserk over a different problem.

_______ a. missing

_______ b. crazy

_______ c. sane

_______ Score 3 points for each correct C answer.

_______ Score 2 points for each correct O answer.

_______ **Total Score:** Using Words Precisely

Enter the four total scores in the spaces below, and add them together to find your Reading Comprehension Score. Then record your score on the graph on page 197.

Score	Question Type	Lesson 17
_______	Finding the Main Idea	
_______	Recalling Facts	
_______	Making Inferences	
_______	Using Words Precisely	
_______	**Reading Comprehension Score**	

Author's Approach

Put an X in the box next to the correct answer.

1. What does the author mean by the statement "For 25 minutes she [the elephant] stormed through the midway while trainers and sheriffs chased after her"?

☐ a. The people who owned the midway did not bother to help the trainers and sheriffs.

☐ b. The trainers and sheriffs were incompetent.

☐ c. The elephant was out of control for 25 minutes.

2. Choose the statement below that best explains how the author addresses the opposing point of view in the article.

☐ a. The author points out that elephant keepers and trainers love elephants in spite of their changeable tempers.

☐ b. The author points out that the elephant named Calle didn't like light bulbs flashed in her face.

☐ c. The author explains that elephants don't like to be confined to small spaces for long periods of time.

3. The author probably wrote this article in order to

☐ a. point out the need for laws prohibiting zoos from keeping elephants.

☐ b. inform readers about the explosive temper of elephants.

☐ c. expose the abuse of elephants by zoos.

4. The author tells this story mainly by
- ☐ a. telling different stories about the same topic.
- ☐ b. retelling personal experiences.
- ☐ c. using his or her imagination and creativity.

________ Number of correct answers

Record your personal assessment of your work on the Critical Thinking Chart on page 198.

Summarizing and Paraphrasing

Put an X in the box next to the correct answer.

1. Below are summaries of the article. Choose the summary that says all the most important things about the article but in the fewest words.
- ☐ a. No one knows what set off a 20-year-old elephant named Tyke when she charged into an audience filled with children at a circus. Such behavior is typical of elephants, who are known for their explosive tempers.
- ☐ b. Some zoo officials believe that elephants are just too violent to be kept in zoos; they say that while elephants need human contact for a number of reasons, they are also extremely dangerous.
- ☐ c. A series of examples provides evidence that elephants are unpredictable and often dangerous.

2. Choose the best one-sentence paraphrase for the following sentence from the article:

   "They separated a male elephant and his mate, putting the two in different pens."
- ☐ a. Two elephants were put in separate pens.
- ☐ b. A male elephant and his female mate were separated, and they were put in pens apart from one another.
- ☐ c. The two elephants were placed in a pen that was different from the one they had been living in.

________ Number of correct answers

Record your personal assessment of your work on the Critical Thinking Chart on page 198.

Critical Thinking

Put an X in the box next to the correct answer.

1. Which of the following statements from the article is an opinion rather than a fact?
- ☐ a. "They're the most dangerous animal in the zoo business."
- ☐ b. "After 15 years, the elephant finally snapped."
- ☐ c. "Despite the risks, many elephant trainers regard their elephants as good friends."

2. From what the article told about how difficult it is to keep an elephant, you can predict that

☐ a. elephants will be left in the wild and not taken to zoos anymore.

☐ b. no one will ever choose to work with an elephant again.

☐ c. zoos will take extra care to train their workers who spend time with elephants.

3. What was the effect of the death of the Houston elephant's calf?

☐ a. The elephant became depressed.

☐ b. The elephant threw dirt at her trainer.

☐ c. The elephant stampeded into a group of visitors.

4. How are elephant keepers examples of daredevils?

☐ a. They sometimes make mistakes in how they treat elephants.

☐ b. They consider elephants to be their friends.

☐ c. They willingly do a dangerous job.

5. What did you have to do to answer question 2?

☐ a. find an opinion (what someone thinks about something)

☐ b. make a prediction (what might happen next)

☐ c. find a cause (why something happened)

_________ Number of correct answers

Record your personal assessment of your work on the Critical Thinking Chart on page 198.

Personal Response

I disagree with the author because

____

____

____

____

Self-Assessment

When reading the article, I was having trouble with

____

____

____

____

TOUR DE FRANCE
World-Famous Bicycle Race

The Tour de France may be the toughest, most grueling sporting event in the world. Only a few top athletes dare attempt it and those who do must be superbly conditioned and have immense determination. Even so, not all of the approximately 180 bicycle riders who start the Tour de France each year finish it. Often about one-third of the starting lineup drops out. That's because the race lasts 22 days and requires cyclists to cover nearly 2,300 miles. A lot of awful things can happen along the way. One writer has called the Tour de France "a marathon of torture." Another has termed it "an annual madness."

2 The Tour de France stops for no one. Everything is done on the move. If a rider wants something to eat, a car will pull alongside and someone will hand over a sandwich or a piece of fruit. If a rider suffers a saddle sore, he is usually treated by a doctor while remaining on the bike. If a cyclist needs his gears adjusted, a mechanic hangs out of the car with a wrench and makes the necessary adjustments.

3 If a biker falls too far back he's eliminated from the race, so riders

Riders in the Tour de France bicycle race travel through some pretty rugged countryside.

sometimes keep going even after a serious injury. One rider made a particularly desperate bid to stay in the Tour. He rode three days after suffering a broken collarbone before the pain finally forced him out.

4 The Tour de France is far too nasty and demanding for cyclists to race as individuals. Instead, the riders form teams. Because it costs millions of dollars to maintain a top racing team, each team is backed by some large corporation. The objective of all the teams is to help their best rider win. One way team members accomplish this is by riding ahead of their number-one man and blocking the wind for him. The top rider is then able to "draft" behind until he is ready to make his move. The Spanish cyclist Miguel Indurain, who won the Tour de France five straight times in the 1990s, had eight teammates who helped him win. Being a member of a team makes it even harder to drop out of the race. Any rider who does so is not only letting himself down, he's also letting down his teammates.

5 The Tour de France is full of hazards. Some of the roads are paved with cobblestones. When it rains—and the Tour doesn't stop for rain—these roads become extremely slippery, so that even a little mistake will send a rider sprawling. When one rider falls, he usually takes several others with him. That's because the competitors often race in closely packed groups called "pelotons." Bikers have no time to react if the rider directly in front of them takes a fall. Lacerated arms and legs, broken bones, and swollen joints are all an accepted part of the sport.

6 Heat poses another danger. The Tour de France is held every July, the hottest month of the year. The blistering heat sometimes causes riders to develop stomach problems or raging fevers. On terribly hot days, riders are sprayed with water from hoses in an attempt to cool their body temperatures. Still, sometimes those measures are not enough. In 1967, Tom Simpson of Great Britain died from problems caused by the heat.

7 Occasionally, the spectators themselves can become hazards. Tour fans, of course, cheer on their favorite teams. But, as in other sports, fans sometimes lose their perspective and endanger the competitors. A fan once tried to slow a team from Belgium by throwing pepper in the faces of its riders. Sometimes political groups use the Tour to attract attention to their cause, staging protests that slow down the race. Worse, they have even

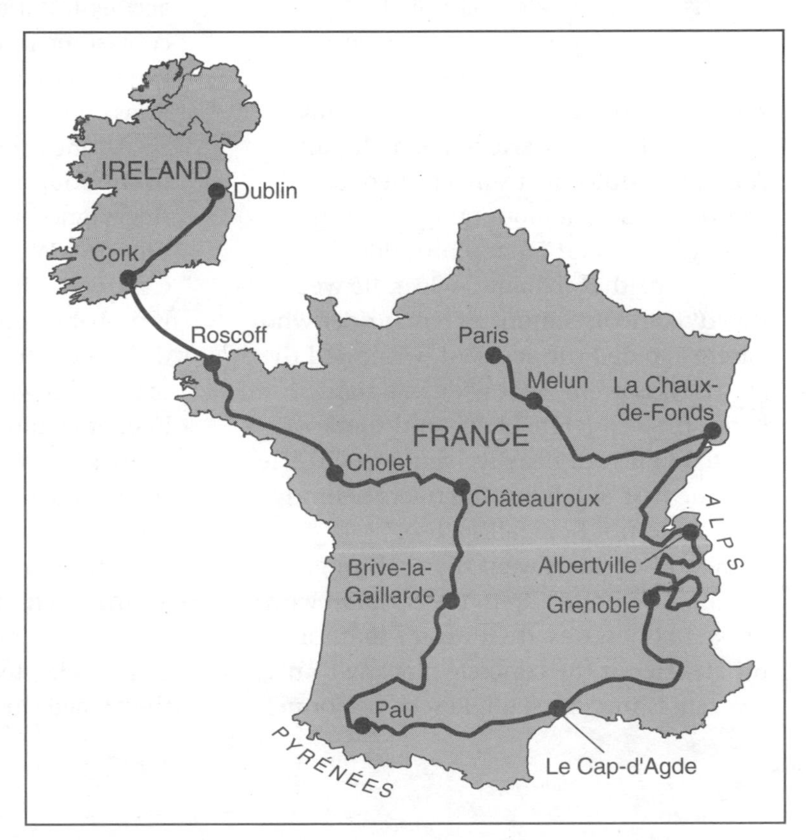

The 1998 Tour de France began in Dublin, Ireland, and finished in Paris, France.

thrown nails onto the road in the path of the riders.

8 The Tour de France covers all sorts of terrain. The riders pedal through large cities such as Paris as well as tiny villages. They zip through the relatively flat wine country, over rolling hills, and up into the French Alps and the Pyrénées. The Tour de France is frequently won or lost in these mountains. Cyclists must have incredible stamina and leg power to make it up these 6,000-foot peaks on a bike. It's a gut-busting challenge.

9 Perhaps the riskiest part of all, however, is coming down those hairpin turns at 50 or 60 m.p.h. A slight slip at such high speeds can be deadly. On July 18, 1995, Fabio Casartelli, racing for an American Motorola team, crashed. He was descending a mountain pass in the Pyrénées at about 55 m.p.h. Suddenly, for reasons that remain unclear, he went down. Francois Simon, a French rider who barely avoided the accident, witnessed the crash. "Casartelli went wide in a tight bend, hit a concrete block on the side of the road and fell heavily," Simon said. "He was the first to fall but the riders behind him could not help falling too."

10 Six other riders went flying through the air. Two ended up in the hospital with broken bones. Casartelli wasn't that fortunate. He hit the concrete block with his face, smashing his skull. Rescue personnel rushed him by helicopter to the hospital. Three times the young man's heart stopped; only twice could the doctors get it going again. Casartelli was the third rider in the 92-year history of the Tour de France to die.

11 Fabio Casartelli was not wearing a helmet that day, and neither were most of the other riders. The weather was so brutally hot that helmets were very uncomfortable. "With this heat, it's impossible to wear a helmet," explained Jean-Francois Bernard one day after the accident. But even when the weather is cool, some riders don't wear a helmet. "It's not the heat," said French rider Didier Rous, "I just don't like to wear one."

12 At one time, helmets were compulsory in the Tour de France. But so many of the riders ignored the rule that it was finally dropped. Would a helmet have saved Casartelli's life? Doctor Gerard Porte said it probably would not have made a difference. "He didn't have a helmet but the impact was mostly on the face and a helmet wouldn't have helped much."

13 Despite the tragedy, the race continued the next day as scheduled. But, out of respect for Fabio Casartelli, all of the 118 remaining riders agreed not to compete against each other that day. Instead, they pedaled in a solemn procession, shoulder to shoulder, team by team. For 147 miles they biked slowly up and down six hills in the Pyrénées. If any rider fell behind, the others waited for him to catch up. For the final six miles, the Motorola team was allowed to go first. Casartelli's six remaining teammates spread out across the road, a hundred yards ahead of the peloton. Andrea Peron, Casartelli's roommate, was allowed to cross the finish line just ahead of his Motorola teammates.

14 Clearly, the Tour de France is more than a physical ordeal. It can be an extremely dangerous sport. The amazing thing isn't that three riders have died during the race; it's that only three riders have died. To win the Tour de France, a biker has to be a lion going up a mountain and a daredevil coming down.

If you have been timed while reading this article, enter your reading time below. Then turn to the Words-per-Minute Table on page 195 and look up your reading speed (words per minute). Enter your reading speed on the graph on page 196.

Reading Time: Lesson 18

________ : ________

Minutes *Seconds*

A Finding the Main Idea

One statement below expresses the main idea of the article. One statement is too general, or too broad. The other statement explains only part of the article; it is too narrow. Label the statements using the following key:

M—Main Idea **B—Too Broad** **N—Too Narrow**

_______ 1. The Tour de France is like no other bicycle race in the world.

_______ 2. The Tour de France is so difficult a race that three participants have died while competing.

_______ 3. The Tour de France, the 2,300-mile bike race held each year in France, is famous as a grueling test of athletic ability and determination.

_______ Score 15 points for a correct M answer.

_______ Score 5 points for each correct B or N answer.

_______ **Total Score:** Finding the Main Idea

B Recalling Facts

How well do you remember the facts in the article? Put an X in the box next to the answer that correctly completes each statement about the article.

1. The Tour de France lasts

☐ a. 30 days.
☐ b. 22 days.
☐ c. 14 days.

2. In bicycling, when a rider "drafts," he or she

☐ a. makes a quick break for the finish line.
☐ b. rides close behind another rider who blocks the wind for him or her.
☐ c. eats and drinks while still riding.

3. When it rains, cobblestone roads

☐ a. become extremely slippery.
☐ b. fall apart.
☐ c. get muddy.

4. The Tour de France passes through

☐ a. Rome.
☐ b. London.
☐ c. Paris.

5. After cyclist Casartelli died during the 1995 race, other riders

☐ a. rode all the next day without competing.
☐ b. took the next day off in his memory.
☐ c. complained about the route that the race takes.

Score 5 points for each correct answer.

_______ **Total Score:** Recalling Facts

C Making Inferences

When you combine your own experience and information from a text to draw a conclusion that is not directly stated in that text, you are making an inference. Below are five statements that may or may not be inferences based on information in the article. Label the statements using the following key:

C—Correct Inference **F—Faulty Inference**

_______ 1. Many riders who admire the cyclists in the Tour de France probably refuse to wear helmets so they can be like their idols.

_______ 2. The Tour de France would be easier if it didn't include mountains.

_______ 3. Miguel Indurain was an incredibly talented and determined cyclist.

_______ 4. Fans of the Tour de France are better behaved than the fans of almost any other sport.

_______ 5. All the members of each team are outstanding cyclists.

Score 5 points for each correct answer.

_______ **Total Score:** Making Inferences

D Using Words Precisely

Each numbered sentence below contains an underlined word or phrase from the article. Following the sentence are three definitions. One definition is closest to the meaning of the underlined word. One definition is opposite or nearly opposite. Label those two definitions using the following key. Do not label the remaining definition.

C—Closest **O—Opposite or Nearly Opposite**

1. Only a few top athletes dare attempt it and those who do must be <u>superbly</u> conditioned and have immense determination.

_______ a. just barely adequately

_______ b. excellently

_______ c. nervously

2. One rider made a particularly <u>desperate</u> bid to stay in the Tour.

_______ a. extreme or urgent

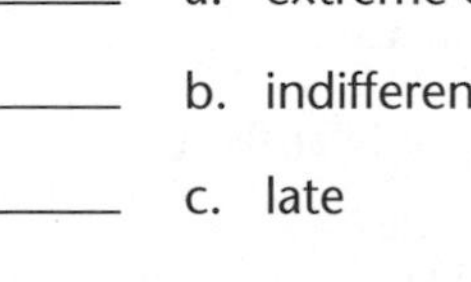

_______ b. indifferent

_______ c. late

3. <u>Lacerated</u> arms and legs, broken bones, and swollen joints are all an accepted part of the sport.

_______ a. healthy and perfect

_______ b. bruised

_______ c. torn and cut

4. At one time, helmets were <u>compulsory</u> in the Tour de France.

_______ a. optional

_______ b. required

_______ c. new

5. Instead, they pedaled in a solemn procession, shoulder to shoulder, team by team.

_______ a. serious

_______ b. long

_______ c. giddy

_______ Score 3 points for each correct C answer.

_______ Score 2 points for each correct O answer.

_______ **Total Score:** Using Words Precisely

Enter the four total scores in the spaces below, and add them together to find your Reading Comprehension Score. Then record your score on the graph on page 197.

Score	Question Type	Lesson 18
_______	Finding the Main Idea	
_______	Recalling Facts	
_______	Making Inferences	
_______	Using Words Precisely	
_______	**Reading Comprehension Score**	

Author's Approach

Put an X in the box next to the correct answer.

1. The author uses the first sentence of the article to

☐ a. inform the reader about the difficulty of the Tour de France.

☐ b. identify some of the riders who have competed in the Tour de France.

☐ c. express his or her dislike of the Tour de France.

2. What is the author's purpose in writing "Tour de France: World-Famous Bicycle Race"?

☐ a. To encourage the reader to take part in the Tour de France

☐ b. To inform the reader about an exciting race

☐ c. To convey a mood of tension

3. Which of the following statements from the article best describes the route that Tour de France participants cycle through?

☐ a. "Heat poses another danger."

☐ b. "The Tour de France covers all sorts of terrain."

☐ c. "A slight slip at such high speeds can be deadly."

4. From the statements below, choose those that you believe the author would agree with.

☐ a. The Tour de France is a test of both body and spirit.

☐ b. The fans of the Tour de France should not interfere with the race.

☐ c. The riders in the Tour de France spend too much time riding their bicycles and should find something more worthwhile to do.

_______ Number of correct answers

Record your personal assessment of your work on the Critical Thinking Chart on page 198.

Summarizing and Paraphrasing

Follow the directions provided for question 1. Put an X in the box next to the correct answer for question 2.

1. Reread paragraph 5 in the article. Below, write a summary of the paragraph in no more than 25 words.

____

____

____

____

Reread your summary and decide whether it covers the important ideas in the paragraph. Next, decide how to shorten the summary to 15 words or less without leaving out any essential information. Write this summary below.

____

____

____

2. Choose the sentence that correctly restates the following sentence from the article:

   "Bikers have no time to react if the rider directly in front of them takes a fall."

☐ a. When riders fall, they affect the riders directly in front of them.

☐ b. If a rider falls, he has no time to react.

☐ c. If the rider in front of you falls, you are not able to react in time to save yourself from falling.

________ Number of correct answers

Record your personal assessment of your work on the Critical Thinking Chart on page 198.

Critical Thinking

Put an X in the box next to the correct answer.

1. Which of the following statements from the article is an opinion rather than a fact?

☐ a. "The Tour de France may be the toughest, most grueling sporting event in the world."

☐ b. "The Tour de France is full of hazards."

☐ c. "The riders pedal through large cities such as Paris as well as tiny villages."

2. Judging by the events in the article, you can predict that the following will happen next:

☐ a. The route of the Tour de France will start to be held in a month that is cooler than July.

☐ b. Riders will be encouraged to wear helmets.

☐ c. The race will be discontinued because it is too dangerous.

3. What was the cause of Tour de France race officials dropping the helmet requirement?

- ☐ a. Most riders refused to wear helmets.
- ☐ b. The officials were sued by the riders.
- ☐ c. It was determined that helmets cause bicycle accidents.

4. If you were an avid bicyclist, how could you use the information in the article to win the Tour de France?

- ☐ a. You could know the exact route of the race from the information in this article.
- ☐ b. Like the riders mentioned in this article, you could refuse to wear a helmet.
- ☐ c. Learning from the cyclists discussed in this article, you could get together a team of good cyclists that you could draft behind.

________ Number of correct answers

Record your personal assessment of your work on the Critical Thinking Chart on page 198.

Personal Response

What would you have done if you were riding in the Tour de France and the rider in front of you fell?

____

____

____

____

Self-Assessment

The part I found most difficult about the article was

____

____

____

____

I found this difficult because

____

____

____

____

FREE DIVING DAREDEVILS

Have you ever tried to see how long you can hold your breath under water? If you're standing waist-deep and you just duck your head in the water, it's not a life-threatening test. Imagine, however, holding your breath and diving hundreds of feet straight down into the ocean. If you descend far enough, the enormous water pressure will start to squeeze you like a lemon and your ear-drums will pound in agony. And, if you aren't extremely careful, you could black out and drown.

2 People have been diving deep into the oceans of the world for thousands of years. As far back as 4,500 B.C., divers in Mesopotamia harvested pearls from the bottom of the sea. Ancient Roman divers scooped up mollusks which were used to produce purple dyes for the Emperor's robes. And people in the Caribbean and the Pacific have been diving to catch fish and lobsters for centuries.

3 These divers were all trying to make a living. Today, however, there is a new breed of depth-defying daredevils who do it for fun. They even challenge each other to see who can go deeper. This underwater

Part-time model and free diver Mehgan Heaney-Grier set a U.S. free-diving record of 165 feet in 1997.

sport is known as free diving and it is definitely *not* recommended for amateurs.

4 In an average year, about 50 people around the world die while trying to see how far down they can dive and still make it back to the surface. The divers, mostly novices, die from blackouts and crushed blood vessels. They don't usually die going down—that's the relatively easy part. They die because they swim back to the surface much too quickly. The body doesn't have time to adjust to rapidly changing water pressure. As a result, internal gases in the body expand too fast, causing the arteries in the heart or lungs to explode.

5 In free diving there are three different ways you can risk your life. One method is so crazy that the free diving federation has refused to recognize new records since 1970, hoping to discourage participants. In this "no-limits" free diving, a diver holds onto a 130-pound "sled." The sled is guided down through the water by a rope. After the diver has descended to a marker set at a predetermined depth, he or she returns to the surface.

6 In 1996, a Cuban no-limits diver named Pipin Ferreras was submerged for two minutes and 35 seconds. He wore nose plugs but no goggles or mask. Ferreras went down 436 feet, 4 inches and survived. That broke the old record of 426 feet, 6 inches set by Humberto Pellizare of Italy. At such depths, water pressure does some pretty unpleasant things to the body. The face becomes wildly contorted and internal organs are squeezed up into the chest cavity. Lungs, compressed to the size of withered apples, have only one-tenth their normal capacity. The pulse drops to the incredibly slow rate of just under 10 beats a minute.

7 As a safety measure, free divers have scuba divers stationed at various depths, ready to offer help if needed. This arrangement saved Ferreras's life when, on one of his free dives, a current carried him away from his original dive site. Although he ended up in shallower water, he was still several hundred feet below the surface. At that depth the water appeared black. Without a mask or flashlight,

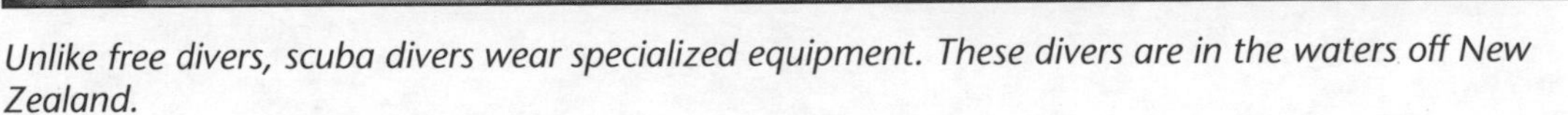

Unlike free divers, scuba divers wear specialized equipment. These divers are in the waters off New Zealand.

Ferreras was effectively blind. Scuba divers had to rush to his aid to keep him from smashing into rocks on the bottom of the ocean floor.

8 A second, slightly less risky, method of free diving is called "variable-weight" diving. In this method, the diver uses a weight of up to one-third his or her body weight. After being pulled down by the weight, the diver discards it and begins the ascent. Because these weights are lighter than underwater sleds, variable-weight divers don't go down as far as no-limits divers.

9 "Constant-weight" diving is a third variation of the sport. This most popular type of dive is done with flippers but no weights so the divers actually have to swim down as well as back up. Although they don't reach the great depths of other free divers, constant-weight divers do rack up some pretty impressive numbers. In the fall of 1997, Umberto Pelizzari set the men's world record for constant-weight diving at 246 feet.

10 Like many other fans of the sport, Jean-Jacques Mayol, a free diving teacher in Florida, thinks that constant-weight diving is the purest test of human diving ability. Scoffs Mayol, "Anybody who can clear his ears and hold his breath for two minutes can set a no-limits record. It doesn't take a whole lot of skill to hang on to something." But Mayol admires constant-weight divers who must conserve their oxygen and strength for the return trip. "They train until every little cell knows how to hold its breath," he says.

11 Although constant-weight divers don't go as deep as their no-limits counterparts, they still face great danger. In 1996, Alejandro Ravelo tried to set the men's constant-weight world record. Just in case he needed help with the last few feet of ascent, he had two safety divers waiting for him at a depth of 40 feet.

12 Ravelo planned to be submerged 135 seconds. But an underwater current caught him by surprise and took him 60 feet off course. He was 15 seconds overdue, a frighteningly long time in a sport where life and death hang on split-second decisions. At last the safety divers spotted him. He was desperately clawing for the surface. Before they could reach him, however, he blacked out.

13 The divers pulled Ravelo to the surface, slapping his face as hard as they could and shouting, "Breathe! Breathe!" A waiting medic slipped an oxygen mask over the diver even before he was out of the water. Ravelo vomited blood into the mask from burst capillaries in his nose. Amazingly, he survived to tell the tale. Even more amazingly, this nearly fatal experience did not discourage him from taking future dives. Saying he would try again in calmer waters, he added, "Even the fish were uncomfortable in the sea that day."

14 Free diving is not an exclusive "men's only" club. There are women free divers, too, all trying to test their own limits. One is an American part-time model named Mehgan Heaney-Grier. She discovered the challenges of free diving in 1995 while on a spearfishing trip with a friend.

15 After diving for just a little over a year, Heaney-Grier set a new U.S. record for women at 155 feet. Then, on August 25, 1997, she went even deeper, setting a new U.S. mark of 165 feet. Heaney-Grier was once asked why she was willing to risk her life to challenge the ocean. "It's a different place to go," she replied. "It's a different place to explore."

If you have been timed while reading this article, enter your reading time below. Then turn to the Words-per-Minute Table on page 195 and look up your reading speed (words per minute). Enter your reading speed on the graph on page 196.

Reading Time: Lesson 19

_______ : _______

Minutes *Seconds*

A Finding the Main Idea

One statement below expresses the main idea of the article. One statement is too general, or too broad. The other statement explains only part of the article; it is too narrow. Label the statements using the following key:

M—Main Idea **B—Too Broad** **N—Too Narrow**

________ 1. In no-limits free diving, the diver, holding onto a 130-pound "sled" descends to a predetermined depth and then rises to the surface.

________ 2. Only excellent swimmers with a touch of daredevil should take up free diving, a sport in which you dive as far as possible and try to come up alive.

________ 3. Free diving is a sport that demands daring and recklessness.

________ Score 15 points for a correct M answer.

________ Score 5 points for each correct B or N answer.

________ **Total Score:** Finding the Main Idea

B Recalling Facts

How well do you remember the facts in the article? Put an X in the box next to the answer that correctly completes each statement about the article.

1. Most deaths associated with free diving happen when the diver

☐ a. rises to the surface too quickly.
☐ b. becomes tangled in air hoses.
☐ c. runs into obstacles on the ocean floor.

2. The record depth for no-limits free diving is

☐ a. 125 feet, 3 inches.
☐ b. 436 feet, 6 inches.
☐ c. 1,004 feet, 9 inches.

3. In case of emergency, free divers

☐ a. attach themselves to boats with cables.
☐ b. carry oxygen tanks.
☐ c. station scuba divers ready to help at various depths.

4. In variable-weight free diving, the diver

☐ a. simply descends as far as possible through his or her own efforts.
☐ b. holds a weight of up to one-third of his or her body weight.
☐ c. carries a 130-pound sled to a predetermined depth.

5. The type of free diving in which the diver descends the farthest is called

☐ a. no-limits free diving.
☐ b. constant-weight free diving.
☐ c. variable-weight free diving.

Score 5 points for each correct answer.

________ **Total Score:** Recalling Facts

C Making Inferences

When you combine your own experience and information from a text to draw a conclusion that is not directly stated in that text, you are making an inference. Below are five statements that may or may not be inferences based on information in the article. Label the statements using the following key:

C—Correct Inference **F—Faulty Inference**

_______ 1. Free divers are the fastest swimmers in the world.

_______ 2. Today, almost no one does free diving in order to make a living.

_______ 3. Free divers have an outstanding ability to hold their breath for long periods of time.

_______ 4. Free divers should never dive alone.

_______ 5. When the body is under great pressure, the heart beats more slowly.

Score 5 points for each correct answer.

_______ **Total Score:** Making Inferences

D Using Words Precisely

Each numbered sentence below contains an underlined word or phrase from the article. Following the sentence are three definitions. One definition is closest to the meaning of the underlined word. One definition is opposite or nearly opposite. Label those two definitions using the following key. Do not label the remaining definition.

C—Closest **O—Opposite or Nearly Opposite**

1. After the diver has descended to a marker set at a predetermined depth, he or she returns to the surface.

_______ a. decided after the fact

_______ b. very extreme

_______ c. decided previously

2. The face becomes wildly contorted and internal organs are squeezed up into the chest cavity.

_______ a. deformed

_______ b. frightening

_______ c. natural and normal

3. Lungs, compressed to the size of withered apples, have only one-tenth of their normal capacity.

_______ a. expanded

_______ b. squeezed

_______ c. compared

4. Scoffs Mayol, "Anybody who can clear his ears and hold his breath for two minutes can set a no-limits record."

_______ a. mocks

_______ b. says

_______ c. praises

5. Free diving is not an exclusive "men's only" club.

_______ a. pampered

_______ b. open to all

_______ c. restricted

_______ Score 3 points for each correct C answer.

_______ Score 2 points for each correct O answer.

_______ **Total Score:** Using Words Precisely

Enter the four total scores in the spaces below, and add them together to find your Reading Comprehension Score. Then record your score on the graph on page 197.

Score	Question Type	Lesson 19
_______	Finding the Main Idea	
_______	Recalling Facts	
_______	Making Inferences	
_______	Using Words Precisely	
_______	**Reading Comprehension Score**	

Author's Approach

Put an X in the box next to the correct answer.

1. What does the author mean by the statement in paragraph 3 "These divers were all trying to make a living"?

☐ a. These divers were more skillful than today's free divers.

☐ b. These divers were greedy and foolish.

☐ c. These divers had a good reason for risking their lives.

2. The main purpose of the first paragraph is to

☐ a. show readers that knowing how to swim is essential.

☐ b. persuade readers to take up free diving.

☐ c. help the reader sympathize with the challenges of free diving.

3. Judging by statements from the article "Free Diving Daredevils," you can conclude that the author wants the reader to think that

☐ a. free divers are taking serious risks when they dive.

☐ b. free diving would probably be a good sport for families on vacation.

☐ c. no one should be allowed to participate in dangerous sports such as free diving.

4. What does the author imply by saying "Even more amazingly, this nearly fatal experience did not discourage him [Ravelo] from taking future dives"?

☐ a. Ravelo does not understand that the diving experience almost killed him.

☐ b. Ravelo must enjoy free diving so much that he ignores what most people would consider to be common sense.

☐ c. Ravelo should be admired and praised for his incredible courage.

________ Number of correct answers Record your personal assessment of your work on the Critical Thinking Chart on page 198.

Summarizing and Paraphrasing

Follow the directions provided for question 1. Put an X in the box next to the correct answer for the other question.

1. Look for the important ideas and events in paragraphs 2 and 3. Summarize those paragraphs in one or two sentences.

____

____

____

2. Read the statement about the article below. Then read the paraphrase of that statement. Choose the reason that best tells why the paraphrase does not say the same thing as the statement.

Statement: Constant-weight divers carry no weights and they Wear flippers to help them swim better.

Paraphrase: Constant-weight divers are not aware of many ways in which modern technology could help them swim better.

☐ a. Paraphrase says too much.

☐ b. Paraphrase doesn't say enough.

☐ c. Paraphrase doesn't agree with the statement about the article.

________ Number of correct answers Record your personal assessment of your work on the Critical Thinking Chart on page 198.

Critical Thinking

Follow the directions provided for questions 1 and 4. Put an X in the box next to the correct answer for questions 2 and 3.

1. For each statement below, write O if it expresses an opinion or write F if it expresses a fact.

_______ a. Variable-weight free divers don't go as deep as no-limit free divers.

_______ b. In 1997, Mehgan Heaney-Grier set the U.S. free diving record of 165 feet.

_______ c. Friends and family members should try to talk free divers out of participating in this dangerous sport.

2. From the article, you can predict that if the world free diving federation decided to recognize new no-limits free diving records,

☐ a. fewer people would participate in no-limits free diving.

☐ b. more people would take up no-limits free diving.

☐ c. no one would do any other kind of free diving.

3. What was the cause of diver Ravelo's difficulties under water in 1996?

☐ a. An underwater current took him off course.

☐ b. He ran into a rock at the bottom of his descent.

☐ c. Waiting divers gave him oxygen when he reached the surface.

4. In which paragraph did you find your information or details to answer question 3?

____

_______ Number of correct answers

Record your personal assessment of your work on the Critical Thinking Chart on page 198.

Personal Response

What was most surprising or interesting to you about this article?

____

____

____

____

Self-Assessment

Which concepts or ideas from the article were difficult to understand?

____

____

____

____

Which were easy to understand?

____

____

____

____

ALISON HARGREAVES
Mountain Climber

Some people called her brave, others called her reckless, and still others called her downright irresponsible. But no one ever called Alison Hargreaves timid. As one of the very best mountain climbers in the world, Hargreaves took on challenges that few others dared tackle. And given the dangers involved, it was not totally surprising when her work led her to an early death.

2 Hargreaves grew up in England, the daughter of two mathematicians. Her parents hoped she would follow in their footsteps, but Hargreaves had different ambitions. She didn't want an academic career. She wanted a life that would push her to the limits of her physical and mental abilities. Such a life, she felt, was best found at the tops of the highest mountains in the world.

3 At the age of 18, Hargreaves left school to become a professional climber. Several years later, she married fellow climber Jim Ballard. In 1988, she achieved one of her long-time goals by climbing the north face of Mount Eiger, one of the highest mountains in the Alps. While most climbers are congratulated for such an

Alison Hargreaves works her way up a mountain with an ice pick in her hand.

achievement, however, Hargreaves was criticized. That's because she was five months pregnant with her first child when she made the climb. People accused her of putting both herself and the baby at risk. Hargreaves responded indignantly to such comments. "What kind of mother would I be if I sacrificed climbing for my children?" she asked. "It's what makes me *me*, and what makes me the good mother that I am."

4 Even after her second child was born, Hargreaves kept climbing. In 1993, she set her sights on a new goal: to become the first person ever to climb the six highest mountains in the Alps in one season. That meant going up Mount Eiger once again, as well as tackling the fearsome Matterhorn.

5 Hargreaves's plan was not only a dangerous proposition; it was also expensive. Alison had trouble finding sponsors to cover the costs. Still, she was determined to find a way. At last, she and her husband sold their house in England and moved to Switzerland. They used money from the sale of the house to finance the expeditions. And in the meantime, the family lived out of the back of an old Land Rover (a sports utility vehicle).

6 Hargreaves accomplished her goal that year, reaching all six summits. But she wasn't finished yet. Two years later, she turned her attention to the Himalayas. She wanted to climb three of the toughest peaks that mountain range had to offer, again doing it all in a single season. The first would be Mount Everest, the tallest mountain in the world; the second would be K2, the world's second-highest mountain; and the last would be India's Mount Kanchenjunga.

7 Saying goodbye to her children, Tom, age 6, and Kate, age 4, Hargreaves headed off on her quest. In May of that year, she sent back triumphant news. She had just become the first woman in history to make it to the top of Mount Everest alone and without oxygen. Only one other person had ever done this before. Most climbers, even the very best ones, use oxygen tanks to supplement the thin air at Mount Everest's summit. Most also employ Sherpa guides to carry their equipment. Hargreaves, however, had reached the 29,028-foot summit unaided. Suddenly she was the most talked-about climber in the world.

8 Hargreaves had no intention of sitting back and enjoying the glory, however; she wanted to push on with her plan. She returned home for a two-week stay with her husband and children, then she flew back to the Himalayas to begin her ascent of K2.

9 K2 is known as the Killer Mountain, and for good reason. One in three climbers who attack its summit ends up dead. The odds for K2 are even worse than for Mount Everest, where one in 10 climbers perishes. What makes K2 so treacherous is its very steep slope and the ferocity and frequency of the storms that

Alison Hargreaves with her children Tom and Katie in 1995

sweep over it. Hargreaves knew the risks, but she wasn't frightened by them. "There is no gain without risk," she said simply.

10 Besides, Hargreaves honestly thought she could handle the mountain. "If I thought it was desperately dangerous," she told a reporter, "I wouldn't do it." Instead, she believed that she had the strength, stamina, and skill to conquer K2. Such an attitude was typical of Hargreaves. Said veteran climber Thor Kieser, "Alison was extremely intense and independent, a very aggressive person on and off the mountain."

11 After climbing up the lower part of K2, Hargreaves and her climbing partners set up a base camp high on the mountain. From that location they would try to reach the summit. Again and again they set out, but each time the weather conditions deteriorated. Each time, Hargreaves and the others were forced to turn back before reaching the top. After almost two months of frustration, Hargreaves was ready to call it quits. It was getting late in the season; soon winter would be moving in and the storms would grow even worse.

12 At the last minute, however, Hargreaves decided to make one more attempt. On August 13, she and nine other climbers left camp determined to get to the summit. Once again, however, heavy winds kicked up. Four climbers, including Peter Hillary, son of famous mountain climber Sir Edmund Hillary, turned back. Hargreaves and five others continued on.

13 Later that day, Hargreaves radioed the base camp with wonderful news. She had reached the top of K2. But as she and her climbing partners headed down the mountain, the winds grew worse. Within an hour, a full-scale blizzard formed, and the already frigid temperatures dropped even lower. The group had no way of sheltering themselves; they had no choice but to keep moving. Back at the base camp, people waited for Hargreaves and the others to arrive. But as time passed, they sensed that something had gone very wrong. Indeed, Alison Hargreaves and the five climbers who were with her never made it back to camp. Later, Hargreaves's coat, harness, and one of her boots were found near the top. Eventually her body was also found. She and the others may have been killed by an avalanche that the storm created. Or they simply may have been blown off the mountain, falling over a cliff to their deaths.

14 The news of Hargreaves's death saddened everyone who had followed her brief but spectacular career. People felt especially bad for the two small children she left behind. Still, husband Jim Ballard was philosophical about her death. "I've been rehearsing this moment for 10 years," he told one reporter. "I suppose what's comforting to me is that she was on her way down—she had conquered K2." Ballard then recalled his wife's favorite saying, which goes like this: "Better to live one day as a tiger than a thousand years as a sheep."

If you have been timed while reading this article, enter your reading time below. Then turn to the Words-per-Minute Table on page 195 and look up your reading speed (words per minute). Enter your reading speed on the graph on page 196.

Reading Time: Lesson 20

_______ : _______

Minutes *Seconds*

A Finding the Main Idea

One statement below expresses the main idea of the article. One statement is too general, or too broad. The other statement explains only part of the article; it is too narrow. Label the statements using the following key:

M—Main Idea **B—Too Broad** **N—Too Narrow**

_______ 1. Alison Hargreaves, a fearless mountain climber, accomplished much in her brief career before she died in an attempt on K2's summit.

_______ 2. When Alison Hargreaves was five months pregnant, she climbed Mount Eiger in the Alps and was subjected to much criticism.

_______ 3. Climbing mountains is considered by many to be the best way to test the limits of one's physical and mental abilities.

_______ Score 15 points for a correct M answer.

_______ Score 5 points for each correct B or N answer.

_______ **Total Score:** Finding the Main Idea

Recalling Facts

How well do you remember the facts in the article? Put an X in the box next to the answer that correctly completes each statement about the article.

1. Hargreaves was born in England, the daughter of two
- ☐ a. miners.
- ☐ b. mathematicians.
- ☐ c. mountain climbers.

2. People criticized Hargreaves for climbing while pregnant because they
- ☐ a. believed it was illegal.
- ☐ b. feared that she was putting herself and the baby in danger for no good reason.
- ☐ c. thought that the pregnancy gave her an unfair advantage.

3. In 1993, Hargreaves climbed six of the highest mountains in the
- ☐ a. Alps.
- ☐ b. Himalayas.
- ☐ c. Rockies.

4. What was most amazing about Hargreaves's conquest of Mount Everest was that she did it
- ☐ a. in the middle of winter.
- ☐ b. before anyone else did.
- ☐ c. alone and without oxygen.

5. As Hargreaves started down K2,
- ☐ a. a blizzard began.
- ☐ b. night fell.
- ☐ c. she fell and twisted her ankle.

Score 5 points for each correct answer.

_______ **Total Score:** Recalling Facts

C Making Inferences

When you combine your own experience and information from a text to draw a conclusion that is not directly stated in that text, you are making an inference. Below are five statements that may or may not be inferences based on information in the article. Label the statements using the following key:

C—Correct Inference **F—Faulty Inference**

_______ 1. Alison Hargreaves's parents were embarrassed that their daughter became a mountain climber instead of following an academic career.

_______ 2. Hargreaves's ideas about the proper behavior for mothers differed from those of most of her countrymen.

_______ 3. Hargreaves's husband hoped that she would stop climbing after tackling the Himalayas.

_______ 4. When Hargreaves climbed Mount Everest, she was in superior physical condition.

_______ 5. No one would ever have heard of Alison Hargreaves if she hadn't died while descending K2.

Score 5 points for each correct answer.

_______ **Total Score:** Making Inferences

D Using Words Precisely

Each numbered sentence below contains an underlined word or phrase from the article. Following the sentence are three definitions. One definition is closest to the meaning of the underlined word. One definition is opposite or nearly opposite. Label those two definitions using the following key. Do not label the remaining definition.

C—Closest **O—Opposite or Nearly Opposite**

1. Some people called her brave, others called her reckless, and still others called her downright irresponsible.

_______ a. flighty

_______ b. cruel

_______ c. stable and serious

2. Hargreaves responded indignantly to such comments.

_______ a. delightedly

_______ b. quickly

_______ c. resentfully

3. Most climbers, even the very best ones, use oxygen tanks to supplement the thin air at Mount Everest's summit.

_______ a. add to

_______ b. display

_______ c. take away from

4. What makes K2 so treacherous is its very steep slope and the ferocity and frequency of the storms that sweep over it.

_______ a. dangerous

_______ b. safe

_______ c. famous

5. Again and again they set out, but each time the weather conditions deteriorated.

_______ a. changed

_______ b. worsened

_______ c. improved

_______ Score 3 points for each correct C answer.

_______ Score 2 points for each correct O answer.

_______ **Total Score:** Using Words Precisely

Enter the four total scores in the spaces below, and add them together to find your Reading Comprehension Score. Then record your score on the graph on page 197.

Score	Question Type	Lesson 20
_______	Finding the Main Idea	
_______	Recalling Facts	
_______	Making Inferences	
_______	Using Words Precisely	
_______	**Reading Comprehension Score**	

Author's Approach

Put an X in the box next to the correct answer.

1. What is the author's purpose in writing "Alison Hargreaves: Mountain Climber"?

☐ a. To inform the reader about a dedicated and determined mountain climber

☐ b. To express an opinion about mountain climbing

☐ c. To convey a mood of fear and foreboding

2. Which of the following statements from the article best describes Alison Hargreaves's overall life goal?

☐ a. "She wanted a life that would push her to the limits of her physical and mental abilities."

☐ b. "In 1993, she set her sights on a new goal: to become the first person ever to climb the six highest mountains in the Alps in one season."

☐ c. "She wanted to climb three of the toughest peaks that mountain range had to offer, again doing it all in a single season."

3. From the statements below, choose those that you believe the author would agree with.

☐ a. Alison Hargreaves should have stayed home with her children instead of climbing mountains.

☐ b. Alison Hargreaves was an unusually courageous and skillful climber.

☐ c. Before she started up K2 for the last time, Alison Hargreaves knew that she would probably not return.

4. What does the author imply by saying "Hargreaves's plan was not only a dangerous proposition; it was also expensive. Alison had trouble finding sponsors to cover the costs"?

- ☐ a. No one believed that Hargreaves was a good climber.
- ☐ b. Hargreaves did not work hard for a living.
- ☐ c. Hargreaves was not a wealthy person.

_________ Number of correct answers

Record your personal assessment of your work on the Critical Thinking Chart on page 198.

Summarizing and Paraphrasing

Put an X in the box next to the correct answer.

1. Below are summaries of the article. Choose the summary that says all the most important things about the article but in the fewest words.

- ☐ a. The mountain called K2 proved to be too much for climber Alison Hargreaves who died there in 1995 after reaching the summit.
- ☐ b. Nothing could persuade Alison Hargreaves to stop mountain climbing, not even the birth of her two children. Before she journeyed to the site of her death, the mountain called K2, she said goodbye to her two young children.
- ☐ c. Alison Hargreaves is remembered as an extraordinarily single-minded and skillful mountain climber who conquered several difficult mountains but whose chosen path eventually led to her death.

2. Choose the sentence that correctly restates the following sentence from the article:

"Better to live one day as a tiger than a thousand years as a sheep."

- ☐ a. Sheep and tigers can never live together in peace.
- ☐ b. Tigers are better than sheep in every way.
- ☐ c. Living even a short time courageously is better than always choosing the safe way of life.

_________ Number of correct answers

Record your personal assessment of your work on the Critical Thinking Chart on page 198.

Critical Thinking

Put an X in the box next to the correct answer for questions 1, 2, and 5. Follow the directions provided for questions 3 and 4.

1. Which of the following statements from the article is an opinion rather than a fact?

- ☐ a. "People accused her of putting both herself and the baby at risk."
- ☐ b. "There is no gain without risk."
- ☐ c. "Four climbers, including Peter Hillary, son of famous mountain climber Sir Edmund Hillary, turned back."

2. From the article, you can predict that if Hargreaves had achieved her goal in the Himalayas, she would have

- ☐ a. begun a mountain climbing school for beginners.
- ☐ b. set a new mountain climbing goal for herself.
- ☐ c. given up mountain climbing.

3. Choose from the letters below to correctly complete the following statement. Write the letters on the lines.

   In the article, ________ and ________ are different.

   a. Alison Hargreaves's position on whether it is permissible to mountain climb while pregnant
   b. Jim Ballard's position on whether it is permissible to mountain climb while pregnant
   c. many of Hargreaves's critics' position on whether it is permissible to mountain climb while pregnant

4. Reread paragraph 13. Then choose from the letters below to correctly complete the following statement. Write the letters on the lines.

   According to paragraph 13, ________ because ________.

   a. Hargreaves's party reached the summit of K2
   b. a sudden blizzard formed on K2 and temperatures dropped
   c. Hargreaves's climbing party found themselves in desperate trouble on the way down K2

5. How is Alison Hargreaves an example of a daredevil?

- ☐ a. She willingly chose to participate in her mountain climbing in spite of its great risks to her safety.
- ☐ b. She became world famous at an early age.
- ☐ c. She took part in an activity that made her feel satisfied and competent.

________ Number of correct answers

Record your personal assessment of your work on the Critical Thinking Chart on page 198.

Personal Response

Describe a time when, like Alison Hargreaves, you were criticized for doing what you thought was best.

____

____

____

____

Self-Assessment

I was confused on question # ________ in section ________ because

____

____

____

____

CLIFF DIVING IN ACAPULCO

Cliff diving in Acapulco, Mexico, is a popular tourist attraction but a dangerous job. Here, a diver soars down to the waters at the foot of La Quebrada.

Each day, at the top of a cliff in Acapulco, Mexico, a group of men stop to say a prayer. You would pray, too, if you were about to take a 130-foot dive into the sea below.

2 The men are the famous Acapulco cliff divers, and each day they astonish a crowd of spectators by diving into water that is a scant 12 feet deep. It doesn't matter how many times the men have done it before; as they approach every dive, they kneel in prayer at the small blue and white shrine of the Virgin of Guadalupe. The shrine, decked out with little candles and paper flowers, stands at the top of the cliff itself. Understandably, the men want a little divine insurance before they step to the edge of the cliff and dive off.

3 Most people would never dream of diving off such a high cliff. But then again, most people wouldn't climb up such a cliff in the first place. To get to the top, divers must scale the sheer rocky face of the cliff called La Quebrada. Once they've reached the top, they walk out onto a rocky ledge and stand watching

the waves roll in and out of the tiny cove 130 feet below. The men are not just admiring the beauty of the sea. They are studying the waves carefully. After all, they must time their dives precisely so that they hit the water when it is at its deepest. The water must be at least 12 feet deep for a safe dive.

4 Although the dive lasts only three seconds, the divers gather enough speed to hit the water going nearly 60 miles per hour. After knifing into the sea, the divers must immediately change direction to avoid smashing into the ocean floor. They quickly loop up toward the surface as soon as they are underwater. Most of the divers are short, with strong, compact bodies. This is one sport where it hurts, literally, to be over six feet. "Tall, lanky people are not the best for this kind of diving," says stocky cliff diver Eustorgio Tornez Moreno. "It helps if you are not too tall because the water is not very deep."

5 La Quebrada has been a hot tourist destination since the 1930s. During that period, Swiss entrepreneur Ernest Henri "Teddy" Stouffer and his movie star wife, Hedy Lamarr, discovered the sleepy port of Acapulco on the Pacific Ocean. Known as "Mr. Acapulco," Stouffer wanted to attract wealthy tourists to his new Hotel Mirador which he built just outside of town. As his top attraction, he hired a group of local men to dive off the nearby cliff of La Quebrada. They've been cliff diving ever since. The tradition has been passed down through families, with sons and nephews picking up where fathers left off. Today the image of the divers plunging into the raging surf has become synonymous with Acapulco itself.

6 The cliff divers at La Quebrada perform five times a day, regardless of the weather. Most of their jumps are done at sunset or at night. Diving in dim light makes for a truly spectacular show because the divers carry a flaming torch in each hand as they go. Tourists can see the divers light their torches, run down the steps to the ocean, swim across the cove, scramble up the cliff, and dive. To add a bit of extra spice, several of the cliff divers will execute a full somersault on the way down. And, just in case anyone gets bored, two or three divers often dive at the same time.

7 To the cliff divers, this is a job—a way of life. They even have their own labor union. The divers, who range in age from 16 to their mid-40s, get paid a fee from the hotel owners and earn additional income by posing for photographs with tourists. Since cliff diving is such a demanding occupation, the divers must

Cliff divers carefully time their 130 foot dives into the tiny cove so the water will be at its deepest when they hit.

stay in top physical condition. Every day they lift weights and run up and down the streets of Acapulco. To protect their act from other daredevils, they do not allow anyone outside the union to dive from La Quebrada.

8 Although they dive off the cliff routinely, the divers realize that theirs is a very risky business. Some say their families refuse to watch them perform because the work is so dangerous. Cliff divers have suffered some terrible injuries, including broken bones, neck and back injuries, and concussions. The torches they carry can leave burns on their hands and arms. But the biggest risk is misjudging the waves and hitting the water at the wrong time. Such a miscalculation will drive a diver's head and face straight into the ocean bottom. "To do this job," explains diver Ernesto Vargas, "you can't be afraid of the ocean. You have to be brave enough to die."

9 Even so, incredibly, no one has ever died on the job at La Quebrada. Maybe the prayers the divers say and the crucifixes they wear explain their spotless record. Or maybe the divers' own fear prevents them from doing anything foolish. "To some of the divers, each time is like the first time," reports Jorge Monico, "You always feel scared—but for this reason, you are always careful."

10 Taken together, the danger, the admiration of the crowd, and the breathtaking setting make cliff diving a thrill even for the seasoned veterans in the group. Asked what it is like to dive off that cliff, a diver named Raul Garcia smiles and says, "[It's] like kissing a girl for the first time."

If you have been timed while reading this article, enter your reading time below. Then turn to the Words-per-Minute Table on page 195 and look up your reading speed (words per minute). Enter your reading speed on the graph on page 196.

Reading Time: Lesson 21

______ : ______

Minutes *Seconds*

A Finding the Main Idea

One statement below expresses the main idea of the article. One statement is too general, or too broad. The other statement explains only part of the article; it is too narrow. Label the statements using the following key:

M—Main Idea **B—Too Broad** **N—Too Narrow**

_______ 1. Local daredevils risk their lives every day to entertain audiences in Acapulco, Mexico.

_______ 2. Each day, outside Acapulco, divers pray to the Virgin of Guadalupe before they step to the edge of the cliff and begin their dives.

_______ 3. Each day, in a show of skill and courage, the Acapulco cliff divers dive off a 130-foot cliff into 12 feet of seawater to the delight of crowds of tourists.

_______ Score 15 points for a correct M answer.

_______ Score 5 points for each correct B or N answer.

_______ **Total Score:** Finding the Main Idea

B Recalling Facts

How well do you remember the facts in the article? Put an X in the box next to the answer that correctly completes each statement about the article.

1. Divers reach the top of the cliff by
   - ☐ a. climbing a steep stone stairway.
   - ☐ b. scaling the sheer face of the cliff.
   - ☐ c. boarding a simple elevator.
2. The name of the cliff is
   - ☐ a. La Quebrada.
   - ☐ b. Acapulco.
   - ☐ c. Guadalupe.
3. Acapulco is located on the
   - ☐ a. Atlantic Ocean.
   - ☐ b. Pacific Ocean.
   - ☐ c. Mediterranean Sea.
4. The cliff divers of Acapulco were made famous by
   - ☐ a. a wealthy newspaperman who moved there.
   - ☐ b. the Chamber of Commerce of Acapulco.
   - ☐ c. a Swiss businessman and his movie star wife.
5. The biggest risk in cliff diving is
   - ☐ a. showing poor form on your dive.
   - ☐ b. burning your arms on the torches.
   - ☐ c. misjudging the waves and hitting when the water is low.

Score 5 points for each correct answer.

_______ **Total Score:** Recalling Facts

C Making Inferences

When you combine your own experience and information from a text to draw a conclusion that is not directly stated in that text, you are making an inference. Below are five statements that may or may not be inferences based on information in the article. Label the statements using the following key:

C—Correct Inference **F—Faulty Inference**

_______ 1. The Acapulco cliff divers are usually religious people.

_______ 2. Most cliff divers perform this trick only for the sheer love of diving.

_______ 3. At the time this article was written, only men were members of the cliff diving union in Acapulco.

_______ 4. If the cliff divers could find any other way of making a living, they would probably give up cliff diving.

_______ 5. Almost anyone could be a successful cliff diver with the proper training.

Score 5 points for each correct answer.

_______ **Total Score:** Making Inferences

D Using Words Precisely

Each numbered sentence below contains an underlined word or phrase from the article. Following the sentence are three definitions. One definition is closest to the meaning of the underlined word. One definition is opposite or nearly opposite. Label those two definitions using the following key. Do not label the remaining definition.

C—Closest **O—Opposite or Nearly Opposite**

1. The men are the famous Acapulco cliff divers, and each day they astonish a crowd of spectators by diving into water that is a scant 12 feet deep.

_______ a. bore

_______ b. amaze

_______ c. entertain

2. To get to the top, divers must scale the sheer rocky face of the cliff called La Quebrada.

_______ a. gradually rising

_______ b. transparent

_______ c. extremely steep

3. Most of the divers are short, with strong, compact bodies.

_______ a. athletic

_______ b. solid

_______ c. loosely packed

4. Today the image of the divers plunging into the raging surf has become synonymous with Acapulco itself.

_______ a. the same as

_______ b. more popular than

_______ c. distinct from

5. Since cliff diving is such a demanding occupation, the divers must stay in top physical condition.

_______ a. precise

_______ b. easy

_______ c. requiring much effort

_______ Score 3 points for each correct C answer.

_______ Score 2 points for each correct O answer.

_______ **Total Score:** Using Words Precisely

Enter the four total scores in the spaces below, and add them together to find your Reading Comprehension Score. Then record your score on the graph on page 197.

Score	Question Type	Lesson 21
_______	Finding the Main Idea	
_______	Recalling Facts	
_______	Making Inferences	
_______	Using Words Precisely	
_______	**Reading Comprehension Score**	

Author's Approach

Put an X in the box next to the correct answer.

1. The main purpose of the first paragraph is to

☐ a. entertain the reader with a humorous anecdote.

☐ b. express an opinion about the cliff divers.

☐ c. introduce the setting of the article.

2. Judging by statements from the article "Cliff Diving in Acapulco," you can conclude that the author wants the reader to think that

☐ a. anyone who dives off a 130-foot cliff is not very smart.

☐ b. the cliff divers put on a good show.

☐ c. cliff diving should be made illegal because it is so dangerous.

3. Choose the statement below that is the weakest argument for becoming a cliff diver in Acapulco.

☐ a. The pay for cliff divers is good.

☐ b. Cliff diving is fun.

☐ c. Cliff divers often suffer broken bones and concussions.

_______ Number of correct answers

Record your personal assessment of your work on the Critical Thinking Chart on page 198.

Summarizing and Paraphrasing

Follow the directions provided for questions 1 and 2. Put an X in the box next to the correct answer for the other question.

1. Complete the following one-sentence summary of the article using the lettered phrases from the phrase bank below. Write the letters on the lines.

Phrase Bank:

a. the dangers of cliff diving and one diver's way of thinking about the sport
b. how cliff diving became a tourist attraction
c. a description of the cliff diving act

The article about "Cliff Diving in Acapulco" begins with ________, goes on to explain ________, and ends with ________.

2. Reread paragraph 4 in the article. Below, write a summary of the paragraph in no more than 25 words.

____

____

____

____

Reread your summary and decide whether it covers the important ideas in the paragraph. Next, decide how to shorten the summary to 15 words or less without leaving out any essential information. Write this summary below.

____

____

3. Choose the best one-sentence paraphrase for the following sentence from the article:

"Today the image of the divers plunging into the raging surf has become synonymous with Acapulco itself."

☐ a. Today, when you think of Acapulco, you automatically picture the cliff divers.

☐ b. Cliff divers are angry that their image has been linked to Acapulco.

☐ c. Today, every time Acapulco is advertised, a picture of the cliff divers is included.

________ Number of correct answers

Record your personal assessment of your work on the Critical Thinking Chart on page 198.

Critical Thinking

Follow the directions provided for questions.

1. For each statement below, write O if it expresses an opinion or write F if it expresses a fact.

_______ a. Wealthy people should find better ways to entertain themselves than by looking at people risking their lives.

_______ b. Cliff divers should allow other people to dive from La Quebrada.

_______ c. The water that the divers land in is only about 12 feet deep.

2. Choose from the letters below to correctly complete the following statement. Write the letters on the lines.

   On the positive side, _________, but on the negative side _________.

   a. cliff divers provide exciting entertainment
   b. cliff divers are often injured
   c. Acapulco is a famous tourist town

3. Choose from the letters below to correctly complete the following statement. Write the letters on the lines.

   According to the article, _________ caused Ernest Stouffer to _________, and the effect was _________.

   a. want more tourists to come to Acapulco
   b. he hired the cliff divers as exciting entertainment for the tourists
   c. Ernest Stouffer's building of a hotel in Acapulco

4. In which paragraph did you find your information or details to answer question 3?

____

_________ Number of correct answers

Record your personal assessment of your work on the Critical Thinking Chart on page 198.

Personal Response

If I were the author, I would add

____

____

____

____

because

____

____

____

____

Self-Assessment

From reading this article, I have learned

____

____

____

____

Compare and Contrast

Think about the articles you read in Unit Three. Choose the four that describe feats that you think would be fun or exciting to attempt. Write the titles of those articles in the first column of the chart below. Use information you learned from the articles to fill in the empty boxes in the chart.

Title	What type of training would you need to accomplish the activity?	What specifically would you enjoy about trying this job or sport?	Which aspects of the activity would you like the least?

People who are not adventurous don't understand why daredevils risk their lives. Pretend that you are one of the daredevils you read about in this unit. Write a paragraph to explain why you continue to take chances. ______________________________

____

Words-per-Minute Table

Unit Three

Directions: If you were timed while reading an article, refer to the Reading Time you recorded in the box at the end of the article. Use this words-per-minute table to determine your reading speed for that article. Then plot your reading speed on the graph on page 196.

Lesson	15	16	17	18	19	20	21	
No. of Words	1110	1035	1197	1219	1131	1155	934	
Minutes and Seconds								*Seconds*
1:30	740	690	798	813	754	770	623	**90**
1:40	666	621	718	731	679	693	560	**100**
1:50	605	565	653	665	617	630	509	**110**
2:00	555	518	599	610	566	578	467	**120**
2:10	512	478	552	563	522	533	431	**130**
2:20	476	444	513	522	485	495	400	**140**
2:30	444	414	479	488	452	462	374	**150**
2:40	416	388	449	457	424	433	350	**160**
2:50	392	365	422	430	399	408	330	**170**
3:00	370	345	399	406	377	385	311	**180**
3:10	351	327	378	385	357	365	295	**190**
3:20	333	311	359	366	339	347	280	**200**
3:30	317	296	342	348	323	330	267	**210**
3:40	303	282	326	332	308	315	255	**220**
3:50	290	270	312	318	295	301	244	**230**
4:00	278	259	299	305	283	289	234	**240**
4:10	266	248	287	293	271	277	224	**250**
4:20	256	239	276	281	261	267	216	**260**
4:30	247	230	266	271	251	257	208	**270**
4:40	238	222	257	261	242	248	200	**280**
4:50	230	214	248	252	234	239	193	**290**
5:00	222	207	239	244	226	231	187	**300**
5:10	215	200	232	236	219	224	181	**310**
5:20	208	194	224	229	212	217	175	**320**
5:30	202	188	218	222	206	210	170	**330**
5:40	196	183	211	215	200	204	165	**340**
5:50	190	177	205	209	194	198	160	**350**
6:00	185	173	200	203	189	193	156	**360**
6:10	180	168	194	198	183	187	151	**370**
6:20	175	163	189	192	179	182	147	**380**
6:30	171	159	184	188	174	178	144	**390**
6:40	167	155	180	183	170	173	140	**400**
6:50	162	151	175	178	166	169	137	**410**
7:00	159	148	171	174	162	165	133	**420**
7:10	155	144	167	170	158	161	130	**430**
7:20	151	141	163	166	154	158	127	**440**
7:30	148	138	160	163	151	154	125	**450**
7:40	145	135	156	159	148	151	122	**460**
7:50	142	132	153	156	144	147	119	**470**
8:00	139	129	150	152	141	144	117	**480**

Plotting Your Progress: Reading Speed

Unit Three

Directions: If you were timed while reading an article, write your words-per-minute rate for that in the box under the number of the lesson. Then plot your reading speed on the graph by putting a small X on the line directly above the number of the lesson, across from the number of words per minute you read. As you mark your speed for each lesson, graph your progress by drawing a line to connect the X's.

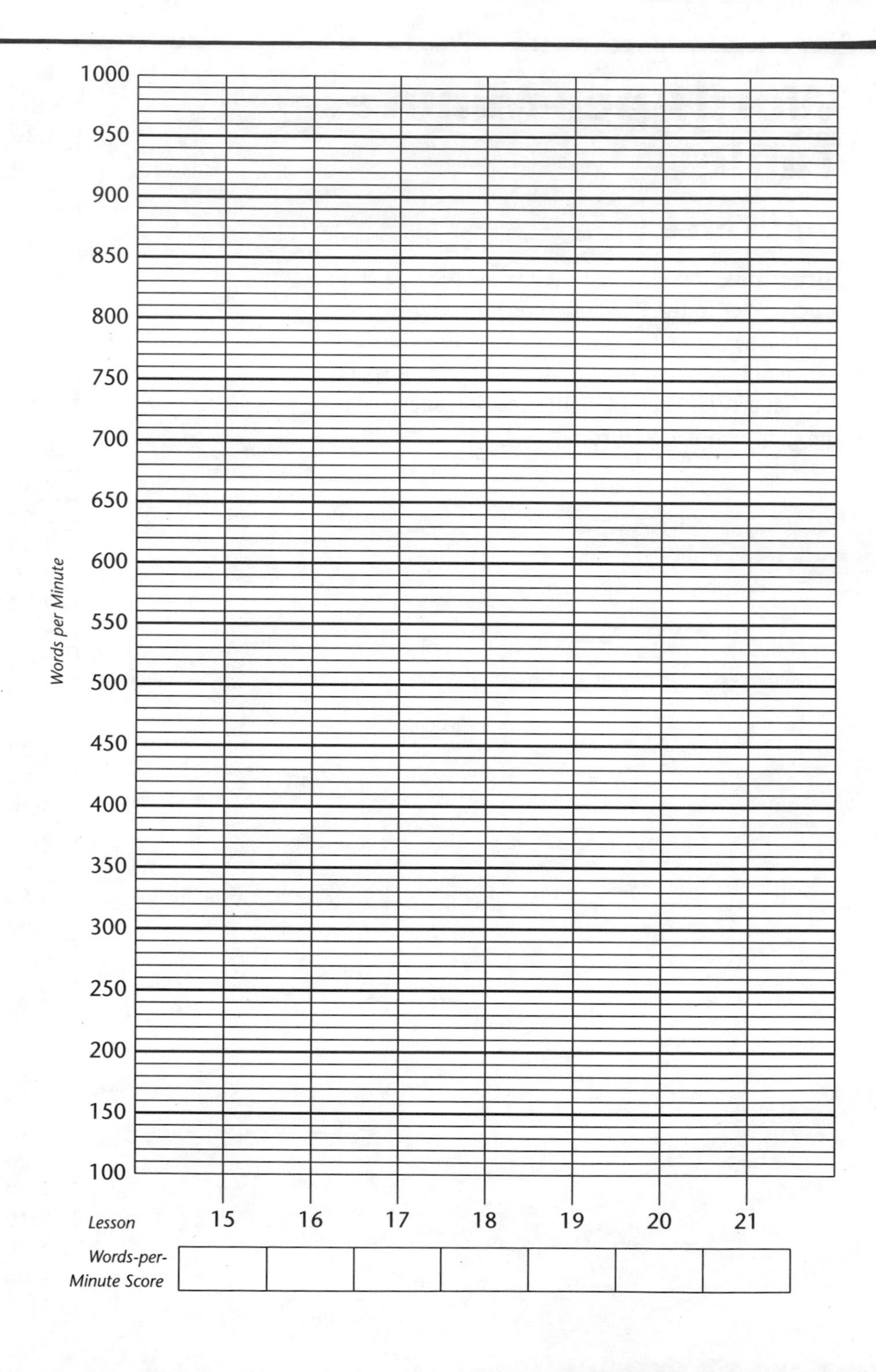

Plotting Your Progress: Reading Comprehension

Unit Three

Directions: Write your Reading Comprehension score for each lesson in the box under the number of the lesson. Then plot your score on the graph by putting a small X on the line directly above the number of the lesson and across from the score you earned. As you mark your score for each lesson, graph your progress by drawing a line to connect the X's.

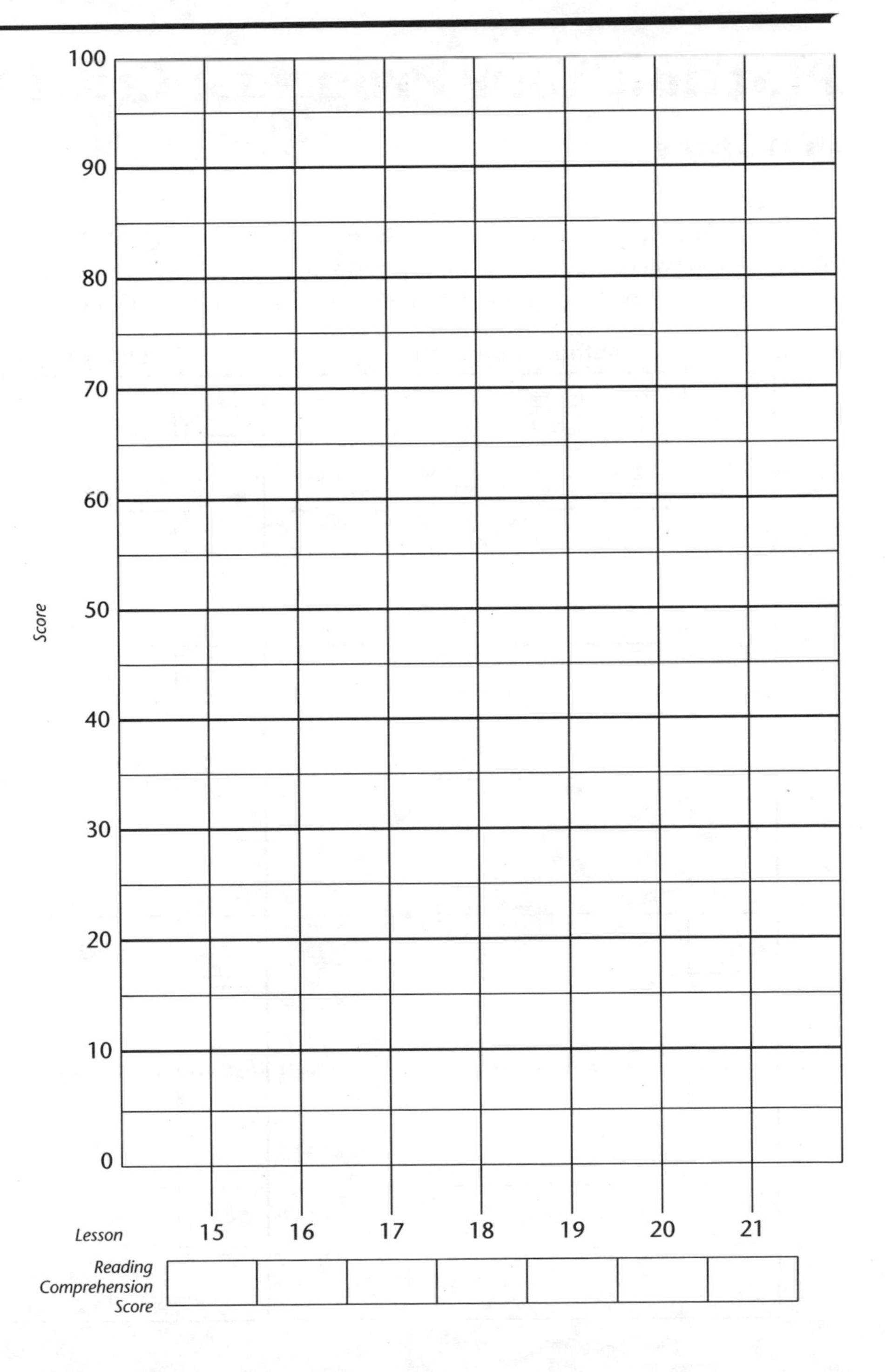

Plotting Your Progress: Critical Thinking

Unit Three

Directions: Work with your teacher to evaluate your responses to the Critical Thinking questions for each lesson. Then fill in the appropriate spaces in the chart below. For each lesson and each type of Critical Thinking question, do the following: Mark a minus sign (–) in the box to indicate areas in which you feel you could improve. Mark a plus sign (+) to indicate areas in which you feel you did well. Mark a minus-slash-plus sign (–/+) to indicate areas in which you had mixed success. Then write any comments you have about your performance, including ideas for improvement.

Lesson	Author's Approach	Summarizing and Paraphrasing	Critical Thinking
15			
16			
17			
18			
19			
20			
21			

Picture Credits

Cover: FPG International © Neil Nissing

Sample Lesson: pp. 3, 4 © G. Brad Lewis/Gamma-Liaison; p. 5 © G. Brad Lewis/Tony Stone Images

Unit 1 Opener: p. 13 UPI/Corbis-Bettmann

Lesson 1: p. 14 © Ron Alston/Gamma-Liaison; p. 15 © J. L. Bulcao/Gamma-Liaison

Lesson 2: p. 22 UPI/Corbis-Bettmann; p. 23 Corbis-Bettmann

Lesson 3: p. 30 © New Line Cinema/The Kobal Collection; p. 31 Dimension Films/Shooting Star

Lesson 4: p. 38 © Uniphoto Picture Agency; p. 39 © ChromoSohm/Sohm from The Stock Market

Lesson 5: p. 46 © Noel Quidu/Gamma-Liaison; p. 47 Gamma-Liaison

Lesson 6: p. 54 © John Van Hasselt/Sygma; p. 55 Archive Photos

Lesson 7: pp. 62, 63 © Peter Brock/Gamma-Liaison

Unit 2 Opener: p. 75 © Michael Montfort/Shooting Star

Lesson 8 pp. 76, 77 AP/Wide World

Lesson 9: p. 84 Mary Evans Picture Library; p. 85 © Sylvain Grandadam/Photo Researchers

Lesson 10: pp. 92, 93 UPI/Corbis-Bettmann

Lesson 11: p. 100 © Ron Wyatt/Sportschrome, Inc.; p. 101 © Shaun Botterill/Allsport

Lesson 12: pp. 108, 109 Chris Noble

Lesson 13: pp. 116, 117 © Michael Montfort/Shooting Star

Lesson 14: pp. 124, 125 Georges Merillon/Gamma-Liaison

Unit 3 Opener: p. 137 © Chip Hires/Gamma-Liaison

Lesson 15: p. 138 © Chip Hires/Gamma-Liaison; p. 139 © Stephane Compoint/Sygma

Lesson 16: p. 146 © Bongarts Photography/Sportschrome; p. 147 AP Photo/Armando Trovati

Lesson 17: p. 154 © Uniphoto Picture Agency; p. 155 © George D. Lepp/Photo Researchers

Lesson 18: p. 162 Jy Ruszniewski/Sportschrome

Lesson 19: p. 170 © Jim Edds; p. 171 © Darryl Torckler/Tony Stone Images

Lesson 20: pp. 178, 179 Archive Photos

Lesson 21: p. 186 © Tony Stone Images/Philip H. Coblentz p. 187 Uniphoto Picture Agency